LANCASHIRE'S ARCHITECTURAL HERITAGE

An Anthology of Fine Buildings

John Champness

Dedication

To my wife, who brought me to Lancashire,
and to my parents and my children,
who taught me the meaning of 'heritage'.

PREFACE

For several years, John Champness, as Conservation Officer within the County Planning Department, has been speaking to groups throughout the County and beyond, kindling in others his own great enthusiasm for Lancashire's Architectural Heritage. In the winter of 1986/87 he was invited by Liverpool University to give a series of extramural lectures on this subject. It seemed an appropriate time to seek to make his knowledge available to a wider public. I invited him, therefore, to put his lecture notes into a more permanent form. The illustrations, which add so much to the pleasure the book gives, are mainly from photographs taken by David Oldroyd, another member of the Department's staff.

Lancashire may lack the great architectural set pieces but it does have a remarkably varied heritage of fine buildings. They add to the quality of life enjoyed by its residents and are an important attraction to the increasing number of tourists drawn to the County. I commend this book to residents and visitors alike in the hope and belief that greater knowledge will lead to greater appreciation.

David Tattersall
County Planning Officer

Text © 1988 by Lancashire County Council Planning
Department

First Published 1989

Designed and published by
Lancashire County Planning Department,
East Cliff,
PRESTON PR1 3EX

Printed in England by Leyland Printing Company, Leyland.

This book was typset by Heckford's Creative Design and Print,
Preston in Berling 10 pt on 12 pt.

ISBN 0 902228 714

Acknowledgements
Most of the photographs in this book were taken by members of
the County Planning Department's staff. We wish, however, to
thank the following photographers for permission to use their
work:

Ian Gibson (LCC Museums)
Harris & Co (Leeds)
Peter Joslin (Heysham)
Stephen Sartin (LCC Museums)
Alan Shelley (LCC Property Services)

front cover: Blackpool Tower

back cover: Gawthorpe Hall

INTRODUCTION

Anyone whose parents have died will understand what I mean by 'heritage'. There comes a time when, after the administration of the will, one has to dispose of a house and the property it contains. Some things one can discard without compunction; other things one keeps because they have a sentimental value which one doubts one's children will share; a third category contains the things which one will cherish, while one lives, and be confident that one's children will be pleased, in due course, to inherit and cherish them in their turn. These things are a person's heritage.

An area, or — rather — the people of an area, can have a heritage too; their **architectural** heritage is that collection of buildings, created by previous generations of inhabitants, and cherished by those now alive in the confident expectation that the next generation will thank them for their care. This book is **my** view of Lancashire's architectural heritage, an anthology of those buildings in the **present administrative** County, which are accessible to the public, and which I find most attractive and interesting.

I am often asked what right I have, as a Londoner by upbringing, to try to define Lancashire's heritage. In response I can only advance three possible justifications: my wife and children are Lancastrians, I have lived in Lancaster since 1975, and my work as the County Council's Conservation Officer takes me the length and breadth of Lancashire to look at its older buildings. Furthermore, since no genuine Lancastrian seems to have had the nerve to write such a book as this, why should not I, as an affectionate outsider, unleash my pen?

I am not attempting to write a history of architecture in the County Palatine, though I hope that by the time you finish this book you will have a rough idea of how buildings developed here, when and why. This last word is the most important because these buildings were built by people for people. They are the shells of dead men and women, of our ancestors, who lived in that foreign country which we call the past; however beautiful they are, they are always more interesting, if we can link them with once real people about whom we know more than just a name.

This book, though its starting point is the pleasure that some buildings have given me, is not the ego-trip of a dilettante, but an invitation to you to share my interest and enthusiasm. It is an invitation to undertake a mental journey in the comfort of your armchair — and later, if you will, a series of real journeys — to look at what I regard as the finest buildings (and their contents) which the present County has to offer. If you don't live in or near Lancashire, I hope that the photographs will help you to make the journey entirely in your head.

A man who writes an anthology gives a hostage to fortune and runs the risk of being criticised for what he chooses to include and what he decides to leave out. I have sought, and am very grateful for, the advice of many architect friends, notably Kevin Eastham and Keith Ingham, and I should also like to thank three historians who have saved me from many errors — Nigel Morgan and Jonathan Ratter, who have compiled most of the Statutory Lists of buildings of special architectural or historic interest in Lancashire, and Colin Stansfield who knows more than any of us about the architects practising here during the last two centuries. But in the end the choices made and the opinions expressed are mine alone. My criteria are simplicity itself: to be included, a building must be accessible and it must be worth travelling to see.

Lancaster Castle and Priory (Peter Joslin)

By implication, any building which I mention carries some sort of recommendation, so how do I qualify my recommendations? A building merely named in normal type is – in my view – only worth looking for if you are already nearby; a building mentioned in **bold type** and then described is worth a détour; a building named in **BOLD CAPITALS** and then described is well worth a special journey, even from outside the County. The Index gives, as well as page numbers, the National Grid reference of all the buildings which are worth a special journey and those which are worth, say, a half-hour détour or which could be the main feature of a half-day out. All these grid references are preceded by the number of the Ordnance Survey Landranger map on which the building is marked; so Blackpool Tower, which is followed in the index by the reference (102/ 306 360), can be found on sheet 102 at the point 306 360.

This book does not mention all the features which you will see when you visit a building. I probably have noticed them, but my space is somewhat limited; and – as the greatest of all propagandists, Voltaire, once wrote – the best way of boring people is to tell them everything. This book is not a guide but a compass, to point you in what I regard as the most interesting directions, so that you can then make as many detailed discoveries as you can or wish. Bon Voyage!

CONTENTS

Chapter One
The Norman Legacy

Sawley Abbey

1. THE NORMAN LEGACY

If one walks over the Loyne Bridge between Gressingham and Hornby, in the heart of the Lune Valley which contains several of the County's most interesting buildings in some of its most attractive scenery, one is suddenly brought face to face with a reminder of a once less pleasant reality: staring down from the Hornby side is the square, concrete-rimmed eye of a 'pill box' placed there in 1939. Fifty yards further on one sees that this ugly little hexagon, designed to guard one of the few bridges over the Lune, is lurking just outside a much more extensive earthen rampart with a tree-clad mound at the further end: this site has, obviously, had military significance for centuries. The earthworks, which are now called the **Castle Stede** at **Hornby,** are all that remains of a 'motte and bailey' castle which was probably built in the 1090s , in a matter of days and doubtless by forced labour, to control what was then merely a ford over the Lune and to serve as a stronghold for a Norman knight and his retinue, as they sought to tighten their grip on the inhospitable no man's land of England's North West Frontier.

There are several such 'castles' in the Lune Valley, notably near the churches at Arkholme, Melling and Halton. The one at Halton may be the earliest because, before the Norman Conquest, the manor of Halton (which then included Lancaster) belonged to Tostig, the Earl of Northumberland, and many of his lands were granted in the 1070s to Roger of Poitou, King William's tenant-in-chief in this area. The 'castle' at Hornby is, however, by far the best preserved, probably because it lies away from a village and was replaced by the stone-built Hornby Castle which stands on a strategically better site. In plan the Castle Stede is an oval enclosure (or bailey), built on a natural spur of a hill, with a circular mound (or motte) which rises perhaps twenty feet above the bailey. Originally the rampart around the bailey would have been topped with a timber palissade to afford further protection, and a wooden tower would have crowned the motte to serve as a last refuge in the case of serious attack.

Such strongholds were introduced to England by the Normans, and the Bayeux Tapestry shows four or five examples. Soon after the Norman landing in 1066 one was built at Hastings to protect the bridgehead, and the Tapestry clearly shows soldiers digging a ditch and building up a mound with layers of rammed earth. Earlier in the story William of Normandy's knights are seen attacking a similar castle at Dinan in Brittany; their success seems to be due to the ease with which they are setting fire to the timber palissade! The future obviously lay with towers and walls of stone, and it is with these stone castles, built perhaps a century after the Norman Conquest, that the continuous story of Lancashire's architectural heritage may be said to begin.

Hornby Castle Stede

Lancashire's finest medieval castle is undoubtedly at Lancaster. Its stone keep cannot, however, be visited because it forms part of Her Majesty's Prison, so the best place to see a keep is at **Clitheroe Castle,** which is a landmark for several miles around and therefore a good vantage point for views along the Ribble Valley and over to the great whale-backed hill of Pendle. The keep at Clitheroe has other claims to fame: it is perhaps the smallest one in England and certainly the only castle remaining in the County which had a Royalist garrison during the Civil War.

The castle we see today, perched on its limestone outcrop, was probably built around 1186 by Robert de Lacy to house and protect the administrative centre of his vast estate, the Honour of Clitheroe, which stretched from Slaidburn to Bury on the western side of the Pennine watershed. The keep stood within a protective wall whose line can be traced on the north and west. Within this bailey there must have been other buildings, probably first built of wood rather than of stone; an old plan shows a stable, a courthouse, a chapel dedicated to St. Michael and the house where the steward of the estate lived. This house now accommodates the Castle Museum which has interesting displays on local history, including the workshops of such traditional craftsmen as printers and clogmakers, as well as a section on the geology of the Ribble Valley area as it can be seen by the motorist.

The rooms in the keep were probably little used, except in times of unrest, because they only measure about twenty feet square. The present entrance in the east wall takes one through what was originally a window into the basement; the original entrance is on the right of the floor above and was reached up an external wooden staircase which no longer survives. In the adjacent corner turret is a now inaccessible spiral staircase which once rose to the floor above and to the battlements.

The castle saw active service during the Civil War when, despite the fact that the Honour of Clitheroe belonged to the King, the people of Clitheroe garrisoned it for Parliament. It was captured by Royalist troops in the summer of 1644, but they departed in some haste six weeks later when they heard of the defeat of Prince Rupert at Marston Moor. Thereafter the republican

government ordered in 1649 that the castle be put, as they wrote, into 'such a condition that it might neither be a charge to the Commonwealth to keep it, nor a danger to have it kept against them'. This tortuously worded order is probably the reason for the gaping hole in the eastern wall — rather than Oliver Cromwell's cannon ball or a stone hurled by a giant on Pendle Hill, as the local legends insist. Be that as it may, the keep was a virtual ruin when it was repaired in 1848, as

Clitheroe Castle

the scale of the repairs, carried out in light-coloured, smooth-faced limestone blocks, clearly shows.

The keep of **Lancaster Castle** is much larger and may be older than the one at Clitheroe. Local legends say that it was built by Roger of Poitou, but it was not; nor was the great gatehouse built by John of Gaunt, even though it bears his name and a statue of him stands above the gateway! Who then built the castle at Lancaster? As is so often the case, the probable explanation is even more interesting than the fanciful one.

Roger of Poitou, a member of the great Norman family of Montgomery who got his nickname because of his wife's large estates in western France, was the most important feudal tenant of William the Conqueror in what we call South and Central Lancashire — although the County was not recognised as an independent administrative unit until 1182. The area north of the Ribble was not even part of the Kingdom of England, but was a no man's land also claimed by the King of Scots.

William Rufus put an end to this uncertainty in 1092, when his army marched down the Eden Valley and captured Carlisle. Thereafter Roger of Poitou, who had helped Rufus, was also given both the Lonsdale and the Furness areas to hold as a second line of defence against a possible Scottish invasion. The administrative centre of the Lune Valley in Anglo-Saxon times had been Halton, but Roger moved his headquarters to Lancaster. It was a place of far greater strategic significance, since it commanded the lowest crossing place on the Lune at the junction of the three main routes from Scotland — around the Cumbrian coast and across the sands of Morecambe Bay, over Shap Fell, or down the Lune Valley — before they continued south across the plain on the west of the Bowland Fells.

Here Roger established a castle within the remains of a Roman fort, first built in AD 79 by Agricola, who had also recognised the strategic importance of Lancaster's site. Roger's castle must have been a motte and bailey, rather than the keep which is associated with his name, because the latter is typical in its size and form of the middle of the twelfth century. It is a three-storey tower about eighty feet square and seventy feet high, with shallow buttresses at the corners

Lancaster Castle (Peter Joslin)

Lancaster Castle — Gatehouse

and half-way along the sides; it is divided internally by a central wall and had an entrance, as at Clitheroe, on the first floor.

If Roger of Poitou did not build the keep, who did? The short answer is that nobody knows. The other most widely canvassed name is, traditionally, that of King John, who during his reign spent the sum of £635.7s.1½d on the castle. This was a sizeable sum in the early thirteenth century but was not enough, as the known costs of other castles show, to build a keep as massive

as the one at Lancaster — quite apart from the fact that it would have been a very old-fashioned design for John, who knew more than most of his contemporaries about up-to-date methods of castle building. John's father, Henry II, is therefore another candidate, but the financial records of his reign, which appear to be complete, make no mention of significant expenditure in Lancaster. If we restrict ourselves, as I think we must, to the mid-twelfth century, that leaves only King Stephen, and King David I of Scots. To my mind, the less probable of the two is Stephen.

When Henry I died in 1135, he wanted his daughter Matilda to succeed him despite her marriage to a French baron, the Earl of Anjou. She was, however, supplanted by her cousin Stephen, who was a grandson of the Conqueror and enjoyed the support of most of the English barons. Matilda invaded England with an army in 1139, and in the 'Civil War' which ensued Stephen bought off the King of Scots (who was fishing in troubled waters by supporting Matilda) by accepting his claim to Cumbria as far south as Lancaster. Between 1141 and 1153, when David died, Lancaster was therefore under Scottish control. David is known to have ordered building work at Carlisle Castle – probably the keep – and it would have made sense for him to strengthen the bridgehead on the southern boundary of his extended kingdom. I doubt that we shall ever know for sure, but the claim for David King of Scots is certainly plausible and has an irony which I for one find appealing.

King John's contribution to the castle is probably visible now only in the inner gateway of 'John of Gaunt's' Gatehouse (whose arch is decorated with the 'dogtooth' moulding typical of the earlier thirteenth century) and in the towers which originally projected forward of the wall, so as to concentrate flanking fire on an attacking enemy. The only one of these which one can still see, though its external masonry looks later than thirteenth-century, is the Well Tower – the one with the eroded stonework to the right of the gatehouse. This is sometimes called the Witches' Tower, because it probably held the Pendle witches during their trial in 1612.

I have already stated that, despite its name and his statue (which only dates from the 1820s) John of Gaunt's Gatehouse was not built by him; who then was the builder? John of Gaunt was without doubt the greatest of the medieval Dukes of Lancaster, the youngest son of Edward III, a claimant to the throne of Castille and one of the richest and most powerful men in the Kingdom during the reign of his nephew Richard II. He was the 'time-honoured Lancaster' mentioned in Shakespeare's play **Richard II,** but he does not appear to have spent more than a fortnight in the town during the whole of his adult life. Nevertheless, the arms of the King of England and his son are carved on the two shields which flank the statue on the gateway, and the mistake was made more than two

Lancaster Castle – John of Gaunt

hundred years ago that these referred to Edward III and John of Gaunt – which would have dated the gateway to the 1360s or 1370s.

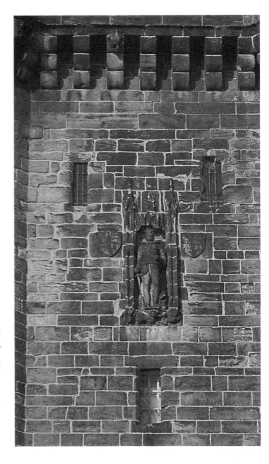

We know that it was a mistake because the royal coats of arms show the three lions of England quartered with **three** French fleurs-de-lys. (This was because at that time the King of England laid claim to the throne of France). However, the arms of the King of France only bore three fleurs-de-lys after 1403, so the gatehouse must have been largely built sometime between 1403 and 1413 when Henry IV died and his son became King as Henry V. This inference is corroborated by the royal accounts which show that between 1402 and 1422 (when Henry V died) more than £2,500 was spent on 'new works' at the castle – enough and more to build the gatehouse.

But why should Henry IV have wanted to build the gatehouse at such expense? He had in fact good reason to strengthen the castle in Lancaster, because the area had been devastated during a Scottish invasion in 1389, and a similar attack would have been a public humiliation for a King who was also the Duke of Lancaster. Henry certainly got his money's worth, because the gatehouse now counts among the finest examples of its type in the country – with its semi-octagonal flanking towers, its portcullis, and its battlements built out on brackets so that missiles could be hurled onto anyone trying to break down the gate. It is in fact not much smaller than the keep and would have fulfilled much the same function.

As I wrote earlier, during the thirteenth century the castle had been surrounded by a wall with projecting towers – but not the ones which one can see today, which date from the early nineteenth-century extensions to the prison which I shall mention in Chapter 7. In such castles the weakest point is, obviously, the gateway, so everything was done to make gatehouses as strong as possible, with the result that in late medieval times they tended to replace the keep as the strongest part of a castle, the refuge of last resort in time of attack and the administrative centre in times of peace. Lancaster's gatehouse is no exception, for its top floor (which measures about sixty feet by fifty feet) contained the constable's living quarters, a courtroom and a chapel, while the lower two floors provided accommodation for men-at-arms.

I am, however, inclined to believe that the gatehouse is as much a political statement as a military necessity. Henry IV was the son of John of Gaunt, the Duke of Lancaster, but he had been exiled because of his political opposition to Richard II. On the death of John of Gaunt in 1399, Richard exiled Henry for life and confiscated his lands and title, a high-handed action which alarmed many of his barons. Henry, who had a reputation as a battle-hardened soldier, invaded Yorkshire with a handful of men in July 1399 and swore an oath at Doncaster that he sought nothing more than his rights and a reform of the government. This won him the allegiance of the major Northern families of the Nevilles and Percies. He then persuaded Richard to negotiate, but took him prisoner at Flint and transferred him to the Tower of London. Despite his oath, he then staged a coup d'état in September and was acknowledged to be King by a compliant Parliament. The rightful King Richard was dead by February 1400 in Henry's castle at Pontefract.

The lands of the Duchy of Lancaster became once more part of the royal domain, and since that time the reigning monarch has also been the Duke of Lancaster – thus

prompting the Lancastrians' proud and distinctive reply to the Loyal Toast. Henry IV had every incentive to play down his treachery and usurpation and to bolster his claim that the Duke of Lancaster was by right the King of England. How better to do this than with an ostentatious symbol of his kingly power in the town from which his Duchy got its name? It is impressive enough today and still used as a trademark of the town, but it must have been even more imposing when most men lived in single-storey huts, and the only stone buildings in most of the County were churches without architectural pretensions.

Lancaster Priory

A stone's throw to the north of Lancaster Castle stands St. Mary's church, now commonly known as **Lancaster Priory**. This courtesy title was not adopted until the 1930s, but it does serve as a reminder that the first monastery in Lancashire stood on its site and that the Norman Conquest of England was also a sort of crusade. In the eyes of eleventh-century Europeans the Church in England was ignorant, ill-organised and badly in need of reform, and so in every centre of importance Norman landowners established monasteries in the hope of improving the quality of religious observance. The monastery in Lancaster was founded in 1094 by none other than Roger of Poitou; it was a priory of Benedictine monks (so called because they followed a rule of life written by St. Benedict) and they were subordinate to the Abbot of St. Martin's Abbey at Sées in Normandy, which had been founded by Roger's father. This was to lead to problems during the Hundred Years' War, but in 1094 meant, at least in Roger's mind, that the services would be well and duly sung to the honour of God, and that He would therefore listen with greater attention to the prayers offered by the monks for the salvation of the souls of Roger himself and his family. Nothing certainly of Roger's time is now visible above the ground, so I shall describe the church in the next chapter.

The only monastic church still standing in Lancashire is the **Priory** right at the other end of the County at **Upholland.** It was built around 1330 by the Bishop of Lichfield, in whose diocese Lancashire south of the Ribble was included until the creation of the diocese of Chester in 1541. The nave of the present church was the monks' choir, and the present

Canons — who were ordained priests, not monks, living according to a rule which was similar to that of the Benedictines — was founded around 1190 at Burscough. Two pillars of the church, which was rebuilt about a hundred years later, can be seen at the edge of a caravan park, but the most interesting fact about the church is that it was the burial place of the Stanley family of Lathom. They were the major landowners in the south of the County, and their promotion to the nobility came in 1485 when Thomas Stanley was created Earl of Derby by his grateful stepson Henry VII, after he had betrayed Richard III by changing sides during the battle of Bosworth. After the Dissolution of

Upholland Priory

chancel only dates from 1882. The tower was built in the later fifteenth century on a smaller scale than originally intended. It is therefore something of an anticlimax, but the present nave is a spacious and quite stately building with boldly moulded pillars and arches and tall windows in the aisles. There is nothing to suggest that an upper tier of windows, called clearstorey windows, was ever built above the arches — though they may have been planned, since the church would certainly have been more impressive with them, as one can see at Lancaster Priory. Upholland Priory must always have looked much as it does today, except that all the rubble stonework would have been plastered, limewashed and probably painted.

The only other monastic buildings in the County are, unfortunately, ruins and not very imposing at that. A priory of Augustinian

the Monasteries in 1539 at least three of the Derby monuments were taken to Ormskirk parish church (where they can be seen in the south-east chapel) and the bells of the priory church were hung in a special tower built at Ormskirk church to house them.

The Earl of Derby had promised to maintain a priest at Burscough if his family chapel were spared, but his wish was not granted. Another monastic building does survive, however, in Lancashire because it was used as the burial place of a gentry family: this is the former Chapter House of **Cockersand Abbey.** This abbey too was founded in about 1190, a few years after a saintly hermit had established a leper hospital on the bleak and windswept site on the edge of the Irish Sea. It was colonised by Premonstratensian Canons (much the same as Augustinians) from Croxton Abbey in

Cockersand Abbey

Leicestershire. At the time of the Dissolution the abbey's site and neighbouring estate were bought from Henry VIII by a gentleman from Pilling whose daughter, Anne, later married Robert Dalton of Thurnham Hall and brought him the Cockersand estate as her dowry.

Like many gentry families in the western parts of Lancashire in Elizabethan times and later the Daltons were, despite the inconvenience and occasional dangers, more or less open in practising the traditional Catholic religion. They demolished most of the monastery buildings, but retained the early thirteenth-century Chapter House and used it as the family mausoleum for several generations. The Chapter House — which is so called because it is where the canons discussed the daily business of the monastery after reading aloud a chapter from their Rule — is best approached along the coastal path from Glasson Dock. It is often closed, so one has to be prepared for a disappointment and choose a fine day, in order to have the consolation of the views north-west across Morecambe Bay and east to the Bowland Fells. If the door is open, it reveals a beautiful octagonal room with deeply moulded vaulting ribs springing from a central pillar whose capital is delicately carved with leaves. Two treasures, which perhaps came from Cockersand Abbey, can now be seen in Lancaster Priory Church — a splendid carved chest with Renaissance details in the

regimental chapel, and the fourteenth-century choir stalls.

The Premonstratensians preferred sites which were far from towns and from the distractions of the secular world, but the monks best known for their aversion to the 'world' and for their deliberate choice of sites which were remote from the comings and goings of people were the Cistercians. They followed the Benedictine rule in its strictest possible interpretation and forbade any architectural display in their churches, at least at first. Another peculiarity of the Cistercians was that their Order was organised in a very hierarchical way, with every individual monastery being responsible to another (normally the one from which it was originally colonised) all the way up the line to the Abbot of Cîteaux in Burgundy, where the Order was founded. Another characteristic, which also had architectural consequences, was the division of the Cistercians into choir monks, who spent more time in the service of God, and lay brothers who carried out most of the manual work necessary to maintain the community.

There are remains of two Cistercian houses in Lancashire, at Sawley and at Whalley, both within a few miles of Clitheroe in the Ribble Valley. Neither can compare with the splendours of the great Yorkshire abbeys like Fountains or Kirkstall, but both are of interest and worth a visit.

Sawley Abbey was founded first, in 1148 by a colony of monks from Newminster (in Northumberland) which was itself a daughter-house of Fountains. Sawley was never a rich house: the area was relatively poor, and the establishment of Whalley Abbey later increased its economic difficulties. The first thing one sees nowadays is an arch by the roadside, but this was built up of fragments in the mid-nineteenth century. Of the church itself very little remains except foundations which show that the original austere choir was widened and lengthened in the fifteenth century and that, about the same time, the nave (which had originally accommodated the lay brothers) was greatly shortened. Lay brothers declined in numbers in all Cistercian houses, and their manual work was done by paid servants. At Sawley there were ten in 1148, in addition to the twelve choir monks, but only two in 1381, when there were fifteen monks.

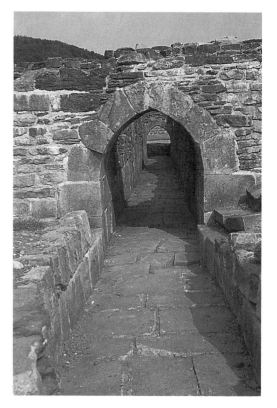

Sawley Abbey – Drain

Another feature of the church is the staircase in the south transept, by which the monks came down from their dormitory to sing the services of Mattins at midnight and Prime at about 6am. To the south of the site the most noticeable structure among the foundations is the great drain, along which water from the river was diverted to wash away the refuse from the kitchens and the latrines which were placed on the far side of

Sawley Abbey – Staircase

the cloister away from the church. I don't know who first coined the maxim 'Cleanliness is next to Godliness', but medieval monks were among the first to practise it.

Whalley Abbey was the last monastic church to be built in Lancashire, well into the fourteenth century. The community was, however, founded in 1172 at Stanlow in Cheshire. The monks found the site on the edge of the Mersey too marshy and inhospitable and so in 1283 they asked the Pope's permission to move. They owned land already in North East Lancashire, and Henry de Lacy (the third Earl of Lincoln and a descendant of the founder of Clitheroe Castle) promised them 'in due course' the rectory of Whalley, that is the estate whose rents provided a sizeable income to the rector and paid for the upkeep of the parish church. The rector did not die until 1295, and twenty monks arrived the year after. For reasons which are unclear, it seems that work was not begun on the earliest surviving building, the great gatehouse which stands near the railway viaduct, until the 1320s. Thereafter the foundation stone of the church was laid in 1330, but the first Mass was not sung in the completed choir until 1380. The High Altar is marked by a large block of stone, but virtually nothing remains of the medieval church except foundations, though the accommodation of the monks is relatively well preserved in parts. The fifteenth-century

Whalley Abbey – Chapter House

canopied choir stalls in which the monks stood to sing their services can now be seen in the adjacent parish church, which is described in the next chapter; and it is said that the abbey bells now hang in the medieval tower of Downham Church.

Immediately to the south of the abbey church is the cloister where the monks spent most of the daylight hours – when they were not in church – in private study or prayer. Originally it had a lean-to roof supported by pillars on a low stone wall which ran around the lawn. The most attractive feature of the cloister is the doorway in the east wall which marks the entry to the vestibule of the chapter house: it has three rows of stylised flowers in the jambs and carved hoodmoulds over the windows on either side. All the

carefully dressed stone stands slightly proud of the rest of the masonry, which shows that the rubble was originally rendered with plaster to give a smooth surface, which was then limewashed.

If one goes through this doorway, one comes into the long undercroft, above which was the monks' dormitory. On the left of the first floor at the right-hand (or southern) end are the impressive remains of the monks' latrines - as at Sawley the drain ran underground along the southern edge of the site, the water having powered the abbey corn-mill before removing any unwanted material. On the south wall of the cloister is a shallow arched recess for the trough where the monks washed their hands before going into the refectory for their two daily meals.

The west side of the cloister is, unfortunately, cut off from the rest of the Abbey site by a relatively recent wall, behind which stands the fine two-storey building, completed in 1415 to contain a storehouse on the ground floor and the lay brothers' dormitory on the first floor. Having been used as a barn for two or three hundred years, the building now serves as the large parish hall for the Roman Catholic community in Whalley. There are, however, hopes (which I share) that the wall will eventually be pulled down, that the Catholic church and hall will be accommodated on the ground floor, leaving space on the first floor for a museum and interpretation centre from which almost all the Abbey site will be visible.

The extensive building to the east of the cloister, which originally had its own separate entrance through the imposing battlemented gatehouse near the parish church — now the only entrance to the Abbey ruins — is what remains of the abbot's house. This was probably begun in the early 1500s by the last Abbot, John Paslew, but was largely rebuilt in the mid-seventeenth century and then again two hundred years later. It cannot now be visited, because it is a conference and retreat centre for the Diocese of Blackburn, but the Hall has a fine roof with heavily moulded timbers which probably dates from Paslew's time. The Abbot of Whalley was an important man in the North West and lived, literally, like a lord.

Whalley Abbey – Gatehouse

Some of the Abbey's wealth and the magnificence which it created can be guessed at from the remains of the buildings, but the best place to see a hint of the splendour of the church and its ceremonial – because by the fifteenth century the Cistercians had lost their fervour for austerity – is Towneley Hall at Burnley. I shall write about the house in Chapter 4, but it contains a good museum which counts among its treasures two priests' vestments which are virtually unique in England. These were made in the early fifteenth century from Italian cloth of gold woven with a pattern of strawberries, on which were sewn decorative bands of what was called **opus anglicanum** (or English work). These are embroideries worked with exquisite delicacy by English craftsmen using coloured silks and silver threads to represent scenes from Biblical stories, like Christ's birth and the Adoration of the Three Wise Men. It is easy to understand why such work was exported all over Europe in medieval times.

The histories of Sawley and Whalley Abbeys intertwined for two and a half centuries and then came to a brutally sudden end in 1537. Sawley Abbey had been closed in 1536 on the orders of Henry VIII, but its monks were restored under a new Abbot, William Trafford, by the leaders of a northern rebellion called the Pilgrimage of Grace, which broke out largely in opposition to the religious changes being enforced by the King. The leaders of the rebellion were tricked into submission and taken prisoner. Abbot John Paslew of Whalley had given no active support to the rebellion but, nevertheless, pleaded guilty to high treason at Lancaster on 9 March 1537. He was hanged with Trafford

Whalley Abbey Vestment

on the next day, and his Abbey too was dissolved. With that, the Middle Ages came to an end in Lancashire. A County had been created and fully integrated into England; the King was also the Duke of Lancaster, but he would tolerate no opposition in the County Palatine. The Normans' work was complete.

Chapter Two
Medieval Churches

Halsall

2. MEDIEVAL CHURCHES

Almost in the shadow of the Norman motte at **Halton,** just to the south of the church, stands a tall eleventh-century **Cross** which may in fact be composed of fragments from three or more separate crosses. Whether this is so matters only to specialists; what is more interesting to most people is the lower part of the shaft and the unique carvings on its four faces. Those on the south are the intricate interlaced patterns typical of work influenced by Scandinavian examples, or carved by the descendants of the Vikings who settled in large numbers along the coasts of North West England. Those on the west represent, at the bottom, the Cross with the Risen Christ above it. On the north, however, is a horse which is associated with the complicated scenes carved on the east, which represent episodes in the Norse saga of Sigurd. The details are not important; basically, the story of Sigurd is about the triumph of good over evil. The parallel with the Christian message is obvious, but what does this juxtaposition of Christian and pagan motifs mean? Was the man who paid for the cross to be carved — presumably to mark a place of preaching and worship which was later superseded by a church dedicated to the Anglo-Saxon Saint Wilfrid — making the point that the Christians' God was even more powerful than Woden, or was he merely hedging his spiritual bets?

Halton Cross

We shall never know the answer to these questions, or even if they are appropriate ones. I suspect, however, that the apparently willing co-existence of Norse and Christian mythologies — admittedly, now only visible in what would have been the furthest backwoods of England — was one of the factors which helped to convince the Normans that their conquest was also a crusade; and that, since their God had clearly blessed their enterprise with success, they owed it to Him to re-organise the Church in England. One of the ways of doing this was to establish monasteries, as I described in the previous chapter; another was by the creation of a more ordered system of parishes and parish priests supported by a ten-percent tax on agricultural produce, called the tithe.

In the area of the present County of Lancashire there were, in medieval times, about fifty parishes, clustered largely in the more fertile (and therefore more densely populated) lands of the Lune and Ribble Valleys and of the plains of the Fylde and South West Lancashire. The area to the north of the Ribble was under the spiritual control of the Archbishop of York, while the country to the south came under the jurisdiction of the Bishop of Lichfield. This was a reminder of the days long before the Conquest, when the area south of the Ribble had been part of the Anglo-Saxon kingdom of Mercia, while the northern area had been a no man's land claimed by both the King of Northumbria and the King of Strathclyde. There was no Anglican cathedral in Lancashire (old style) until the creation of the Diocese of Manchester in 1847, and none in the present County before the Diocese of Blackburn was carved out of this in 1926. About fifty churches in the present County have substantial remains of medieval workmanship, and the best of these are the subject of this chapter.

The Normans may well have been dissatisfied with what they found in this part of England, but there were certainly Christian communities in the area. The cross at Halton is by no means the only one still remaining. There are fragments in most churches in the Lune Valley, at Aughton near Ormskirk, in several museums and in Manchester Cathedral. And there are no less than three Anglo-Saxon crosses in the churchyard at Whalley, which was then the centre of a huge parish covering over 250 square miles of the present Ribble Valley, Rossendale, Burnley and Pendle areas.

The only churches with remains from before the Norman Conquest are at **Heysham** — St. Peter's Church which nestles in a fold of the ground in a haven of peace just away from the bustle of Main Street and its holiday

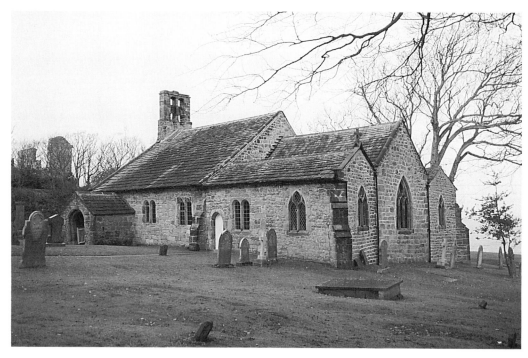

Heysham

makers, and **St. Patrick's Chapel** which stands, patched and roofless, on the windswept cliffs above. Tradition has it that the chapel was built by the saint himself, that is in the fifth century, as a thank-offering for his survival after a shipwreck. I don't suppose that anyone now believes this, but — equally — no-one knows who did build it, or when (though most scholars agree on the ninth century) or whose bodies first lay in the six shallow graves hewn out of the rock a few yards to the west. On a misty morning, or in the light of the sun setting over Morecambe Bay, this can be an almost numinous site, but this is seldom the case; look too far to the left and you can see a holiday camp, the port of Heysham and two nuclear power stations!

St. Peter's Church, Heysham is, like most old churches in Lancashire, more quaint than beautiful with its huddle of low roofs and double bellcote at the west end. When first built, perhaps a thousand years ago, it must have been less than half its present size — a simple, rectangular building, fairly tall and narrow, with a nave at the west end separated by an arch from the shorter chancel where the priest led the worship. This chancel was lengthened in the early fourteenth century, as the curving tracery in the east window and in the now unglazed window between the chancel and the south aisle show. Perhaps 150 years later the south aisle of the nave was added, and then extended halfway along the chancel in the seventeenth century, when the south porch was also built and (I guess) the chancel arch was widened. There are no

written records to confirm these approximate dates (except 1864 for the north aisle); as in most old churches they are assumptions based upon the patterns of window tracery and mouldings on arches.

Heysham — Hogback Tombstone

St. Peter's is famous for its two pre-Conquest stones, a 'hogback' tombstone in the south aisle and the base of a cross-shaft in the churchyard. The hogback, so called from its bowed profile although its ends seem to be bears' heads, originally stood outside in a Christian churchyard, but the men and animals carved on its sides, perhaps in the tenth century, are thought to depict scenes from pagan Norse sagas. The cross-shaft by the entrance to the churchyard may be even older but is more evidently Christian; on one side is a seated figure with a halo, on the other what may be a house with a standing figure apparently wrapped in a shroud. Nobody knows what it represents, but perhaps it is the raising of Lazarus or the Resurrection of Christ; both are appropriate to a religion promising life eternal.

Heysham Church is typical of all the older churches in the County in that it is not in its original form, but has been rebuilt and extended at various times. There are a few remains of churches built in the century after the Norman Conquest – a window at Ormskirk and the lowest stage of the tower at Gisburn – but there is no church in the County which gives a clear picture of the churches which the Normans and their descendants built. The nearest we get to this is **St. Helen's, Overton** which, when seen from the south west, appears as a simple box with a tall bellcote and a south doorway with three layers (or orders) of decorated stonework. In fact the church was extended in a very simple manner to the east in 1771 and to the north in 1836 – with a pulpit and gallery of those respective dates inside – but its rough simplicity is typical of the twelfth century, as is its doorway with its zigzag mouldings and, in the outermost order, some very eroded 'beak-heads', which form a decorative motif looking like birds nibbling at a long sausage.

Tatham

Another church which preserves a fine Norman doorway, with two orders of zigzags and one looking like a well-laid rope, is at Gressingham, while a little further up the Lune valley at Tatham the doorway has a form of beak-head moulding which is almost abstract. The third of these Norman doorways in Lune Valley churches is at Brookhouse – now blocked up and to the north of the tower; this has an order carved with figures which are said to represent Adam and Eve and the serpent. While we are, as it were, in the Lune Valley and of an antiquarian turn of mind, you might like to continue to Claughton parish church, where the larger of the two bells visible in the bellcote bears an inscription dating it to 1296 – which makes it the oldest dated bell in England.

In the course of the Middle Ages almost all churches were rebuilt or extended. There were several reasons for this. The most obvious is that the population grew, albeit slowly, until the Black Death in the mid-fourteenth century, and thus people required bigger churches to accommodate them. The normal way was to build an aisle to the north or south of the nave, by building a new outside wall and breaking through the old one with a row of arches whose shape and mouldings can give a rough indication of when the work was done. Such work was normally done at the expense of the parishioners themselves, but work on the chancel was the responsibility of the rector who received the tithes and also paid the salary to the parish priest. During and after the thirteenth century, when church ceremonial became more complicated, chancels were extended to make them more worthy of the daily miracle of the Mass when, it was believed, the bread and wine offered at the altar by the priest were somehow transformed into the body and blood of Christ. A third reason for extensions, normally in the form of side chapels, was the development in the later Middle Ages of the belief that the souls of people who had died could have their time in Purgatory reduced and thus be speeded Heavenwards, if priests were paid to sing special Masses for them. Needless to say, many people, who could afford to do so, had 'chantry' chapels built for these commemorative services and gave the rents from parts of their estates to pay the priest who sang them.

The finest thirteenth-century church in the County, and indeed one of the most interesting of any date, is **Saint Mary's Church** in a well-treed backwater off the main street at **Whalley.** It stands close to the remains of the Abbey, but is at least a hundred years older, while the ancient sanctity of the site is proven by the three pre-Conquest crosses standing in the churchyard. There must have been a church at Whalley before the present one, because the south doorway has capitals with many scallops which date it to the late twelfth century. The bulk of the present church was probably built around a smaller, older one, with the north aisle being built before the south, because its piers are round and not octagonal. Though the five-light east window probably dates from the fifteenth century and its glass depicting the arms of local families dates from 1816, the chancel from the outside is a

Whalley – Misericord

fine example of thirteenth-century work, with its shallow gabled buttresses and narrow 'lancet' windows; inside, the triple seat for the priest and his servers is probably contemporary, but not in its original position.

Like most churches, St. Mary's is not of one date. The tower, the windows in the aisle walls and the clearstorey windows above the nave arcades were all probably built in the fifteenth century, as were the roofs – the one in the nave being particularly fine. The woodwork is the best part of the inside of Whalley church – not merely the roofs and the seventeenth-century pews but also the screens, especially those around the pews of the rival families, the Nowells of Read Hall and the Starkies of Huntroyde, which stand to the right and left respectively as one looks towards the chancel. The finest woodwork of all is, however, in the spikily canopied choir stalls from the Abbey, datable by the initials W.W. (which stand for Abbot William Whalley) to the years 1418-34. These were altered somewhat in 1866 but are substantially authentic with their detached shafts and vaulted canopies; they also have the finest set of misericords in the County, that is the tip-up seats against which the monks could lean a little while singing their daily, and nightly, services. Their undersides are carved with all manner of motifs, of which only a few are definitely religious. Some are fairly static in their design, but several – like St. George killing the dragon, a fox running

away with a goose, and a woman hitting a man with what looks like a frying pan – are carved in a very spirited fashion. At the west end is a gallery rebuilt in 1813 to carry the superb organ which was originally made for St. Mary's Church, Lancaster in 1728.

In many ways the thirteenth-century chancel of **St. Wilfrid's Church** at **Ribchester** runs Whalley a close second. It has its original lancet windows in the east end and south side, but this south side is disfigured by an inserted Victorian window while, inside the church, the view of the eastern lancets is somewhat spoilt by the heavy tiebeams of the early sixteenth-century chancel roof. Nevertheless, the church has much of interest, and even of beauty, to offer and is well worth a visit on its riverside site. It stands within the earthworks of a Roman fort, whose history is well displayed in the adjacent museum; the foundations of a Roman bath-house can also be seen behind the White Bull public house in the village.

The nave of the church was probably built at the same time as the chancel, as the south-west doorway and the buttresses by the tower indicate. One can see from the lines of stone on the east face of the tower that its roof was originally of a much steeper pitch – as indeed was that of the chancel. Like most towers in Lancashire churches, Ribchester's dates from the late fifteenth century – which must have been a period of some prosperity.

Ribchester

date from around 1500; the nave roof is said to bear the date 1527. Other pieces of woodwork of interest are the seventeenth-century pulpit, the eighteenth-century box pews on the opposite side of the nave and, at the west end, the gallery which is dated 1736 and supported on stone columns which are said to be Roman. Considering where the church stands, this might be true, but I have my doubts.

The interior is one of the lightest in any old Lancashire church, thanks to the ugly dormer windows and the lack of Victorian stained glass. A full-length aisle with octagonal piers was added in the fifteenth century to the south of the nave, and at much the same time its east end was screened off as a chantry chapel, called the Hoghton Quire — presumably after the township in which the estates, whose rents paid for the chantry masses to be sung, were situated. On the north side of the nave is a larger and more interesting chantry chapel, called the Dutton Quire — after another local township — which dates from the first half of the fourteenth century. This has the quatrefoil pillars and heavily moulded capitals, which are typical of that date, and a series of windows (with a few fragments of contemporary glass) which provide almost a text book of tracery design of that period. In the north wall there is a lancet which must have been moved from the wall of the original nave, but the other window has three lights with ogee arches at their head under a flat lintel. To the west the window tracery forms a net-like pattern for which the technical name is 'reticulated', while to the east it forms a complicated pattern of lushly flowing lines.

Churchtown

The roof of the Dutton Quire is almost certainly original, but of a form of construction now very rare in the North West, since it has no beam at the ridge but instead is stiffened along its length by a beam called a collar purlin carried lower down, on brackets at either end and on a 'crown post' in the centre. All the other roofs are more normal in their construction and probably

The **Church** of **St. Helen** at **Churchtown,** which was the parish church of Garstang until St. Thomas' Chapel was built there in 1770, claims to be the 'Cathedral of the Fylde', and I for one would not dispute this. It stands behind sturdy cast-iron railings at the southern end of the now by-passed village, and its tower is something of a landmark in the flat plain of the River Wyre. The church looks late-medieval, but its building history is complicated, as the large number of separate roofs and obvious joints in the masonry show, and goes back at least to the beginning of the thirteenth century — not that mere age is enough to make something worth visiting, at least in my view.

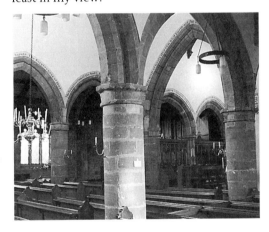

Thanks to the clearstorey windows put in above the nave arcades as late as 1811, St. Helen's is another well-lit church, and the first (though wrong) impression one gets, largely because of the restoration of 1865-8 which unified everything with smooth plasterwork and Biblical texts painted over the arches, is that the church was built in a single campaign. Part of the pleasure of a visit is to begin to unravel the more complicated story which underlies this apparent unity. In its main lines it goes, I think, as follows.

Since there was a vicar here in 1190, there must have been a church before 1200. Despite slight differences between them, the two arcades of the nave appear to me to have been probably built within a few years of each

21

other at about that time; they would have created a fairly large church – a sign of a large congregation or of important status, or both. Perhaps a generation after that, since the mouldings and carving of the capitals are similar to those in the Chapter House at Cockersand, an aisle or chapel was built to the north of the chancel, although this was swallowed up in later alterations. The link with Cockersand is not mere conjecture, since the Abbot was the rector of the parish. The chancel arch appears to have been the next major element to be built, in about 1325, but any extensions to the chancel (which this implies) have also disappeared. There are, however, two early fourteenth-century windows at the west end of the nave aisles, which may have come from the chancel. To the south of the chancel arch is an opening in which the underside of a spiral staircase can be seen. This would have led before the Reformation to the rood-loft, that is, the gallery which carried statues of Christ on the Cross flanked by St. Mary and St. John, but these were taken down as superstitious idols in the 1540s.

From the outside the church looks largely fifteenth-century, and this is because the tower, which is unusual in having a little stone spire to crown the top of its staircase turret, dates from that time, as do most of the windows in the aisles. Two parts of the building, which are obviously not of the fifteenth century, are the hearse-house by the south porch (which is dated 1754) and the two-storey vestry which was added in 1570; since this is so clumsily joined to the rest of the church, it probably was merely rebuilt here, having been bought ready-made elsewhere – the obvious source is Cockersand. The finest aisle windows are those of the Lady Chapel which was built out to the south of the south aisle at the expense of Margaret Rigmaden, who lived up the Wyre valley at Woodacre. It has a good roof, which is dated 1529, and also some interesting seventeenth - century wall paintings with Biblical texts set in scrolly frames. They are now unique in the County, but such decoration was normal 350 years ago. The roof in the chancel is dated 1620 and bears an inscription saying that it was paid for by Sir Robert Bindloss (of Borwick Hall); he had purchased the rectory of Garstang and thus the right to receive the major tithes, but also the responsibility of maintaining the chancel. The roof of the nave looks similar and was probably built at the same time. The fine chandelier was presented in 1746.

Some churches are more interesting for their fittings than for their architecture, and a good example of this is **All Hallows Church** at **Great Mitton,** which has the finest collection of tombs in the County. It is an unpretentious church without aisles set in a quiet graveyard on a bluff overlooking the Ribble, with a fine view towards Pendle Hill. But before one goes inside, it is well worth while walking around to the south side, for here is a fourteenth-century circular cross-head, so fine that I am always surprised to find it outside at the mercy of the elements. It is set on a modern shaft to face roughly east and west, so the best view of one side is in the morning, and of the other after lunch. On the east side within a hexagonal frame is the single figure of Christ crucified, while on the other a canopied framework surrounds Christ on the Cross flanked by St. Mary and St. John, such as one would have found on a rood-loft in a church.

Great Mitton

The church dates from the late thirteenth century, as the Y-shaped tracery in the window indicates. The prettiest feature of that date is in the chancel – the triple seat for the priest and his servers, with its trefoiled heads and decoration of carved flowers. Immediately to the east is a smaller niche which is called a piscina. This is where in medieval times the priest would rinse out the chalice in which the wine had been distributed during the Mass and then let the water and wine (which was believed to be the blood of Christ) drain away into the consecrated ground of the churchyard. The chancel screen through which one must pass to see all this is also worth more than a second glance: the bottom half is late-medieval, with the figures in the doors representing the angel Gabriel announcing to Mary that she would have a son called Jesus. It probably came from Sawley Abbey, since the Latin inscription relates to a fifteenth-century abbot, but much of the upper part is Victorian cast iron.

The finest feature of the church is the Shireburne Chapel which projects to the north and is approached from the chancel through a pretty Elizabethan screen. It was probably built originally as a chantry but was rebuilt in 1594 as the family burial chapel by Sir Richard Shireburne, who was also building Stonyhurst. He had the misfortune to die in the same year, and it looks as though the old roof was used, unchanged, on the new building, since some of the supports are set above, rather than between, the windows. Be that as it may, it is the monuments rather than the roof which are worth looking at. They range in date from the somewhat damaged effigy of a fifteenth-century knight to fine mid-eighteenth-century wall tablets. The grandest is undoubtedly the alabaster memorial to Sir Richard and his wife Maud, which stands more or less in the centre. They lie there, stiffly on their backs in the medieval manner, he in armour, she in a rich gown whose petticoats show that the memorial was once painted. Beneath them on the tomb-chest itself are figures of their children and the coats of arms of the various families with whom the Shireburnes had intermarried in previous generations. On the wall between the windows stands another alabaster monument to the next generation, to another Richard, who died in 1628, and his wife Anne. They face each other, kneeling at a prayer desk, set within an arch flanked by two pairs of 'Corinthian' columns carrying a full achievement of arms and two obelisks to symbolise immortality. Below the couple, to the right, there are kneeling figures of their surviving sons and daughter and, to the left, their three children who had already died, one as a baby.

All of the monuments so far seen are typically up-to-date for their time, but the next three were old-fashioned when they were made in the 1690s by William Stanton of London. He was one of the more famous sculptors of his time, and the effigies are finely carved and elegant in their recumbent posture. The conservatism of the models is doubtless due to the wishes of his patron, Isabel Shireburne, who perhaps saw herself as the last of the line. The second Richard (who died in 1628) had a son, Richard, who lies beneath him and died in 1669. He had a son Richard (the fourth of that name) who died in 1689 and lies in front of his wife Isabel, who commissioned the tombs. She did not die until 1693, but their son had died in 1690 without any children. Isabel was not quite the end of the line, however; the tragedy had one more act to play out. The fourth Richard had a brother, Nicholas, who was made a baronet by James II and came to live at Stonyhurst, where he transformed the gardens. He had a son, Richard, and a daughter, Mary; but the little boy died, aged 9, in 1702 after eating poisonous berries. In the tall monument against the west wall (by William Stanton's son, Edward) he is shown startled at the sight of a skull and some bones, while cherubs weep beside him. The architectural treatment is completely up-to-date in the grand manner with 'Corinthian' pilasters supporting a segmental pediment beneath which are more cherubs' heads.

Young Richard's sister Mary later married the eighth Duke of Norfolk but, when her husband died, she moved back to Stonyhurst where she lived out her life with an old friend Peregrine Widdrington. They are commemorated, as are her parents, in tablets on the east wall of the chapel; the inscriptions are in English and make interesting reading.

As we move through time to the later fourteenth century, we come to the first church which is not merely pleasing or archaeologically interesting, but aesthetically impressive as well, and that is **St. Cuthbert's** in **Halsall** in the far south-west of the County. It stands on a slight rise to the east of Halsall Moss, and its distinctive spire (which is 128 feet high) has been a landmark for more than five centuries. The actual spire was rebuilt in 1852 to a profile slightly different from the original one, but the basic design of the tower and spire probably dates from around 1400. In rising from a square base through an octagonal bell chamber, it is similar to two others at the nearby churches of Aughton and Ormskirk. All may well have been built by the same team of masons or within a few years of each other, but there is no documentary evidence. Projecting from the tower and half-hiding the porch is the former grammar school, founded by Edward Halsall in 1593. It was originally a two-storey building, but was prettily altered in the early nineteenth century.

The church itself is older than the tower, as one would expect: one needs accommodation for people before bells. The nave appears to have been built sometime after about 1325 with a four-bay arcade on either side, and the arches are similar in profile to the chancel arch at Ribchester. Unfortunately, there are no clearstorey windows and plenty of Victorian glass, so the building is fairly dark, and it is difficult to appreciate the fine quality of the stonework. Opposite the pulpit there is a window on the upper wall which some people claim was inserted to light the rood loft, of which one can see the door immediately below. To my eyes, however, the window does not look medieval, and I surmise that it was placed there to allow a Georgian parson to read his sermons with greater ease.

The chancel may well have been built at the same time as the nave, but was largely rebuilt in the later fourteenth century. It has older features inside, like the splendid early fourteenth-century vestry door, on which the vertical joints between the outer layer of planks are covered by wooden mouldings which continue upwards into a display of reticulated tracery; there is also the canopied recess on the north side which now contains the shortened alabaster effigy of a priest. Another fine tomb is on the other side of the chancel, bearing effigies of Sir Henry Halsall (who died in 1523) and his wife Margaret Stanley; they are in plain alabaster, but the shields below them have recently been repainted.

It must be admitted that, though it has some interesting details, the chancel is rather dark – in part because it has no windows on the north side – and really looks finer from the outside. Here one can see how well integrated a design it is, with its tall three-light windows between deep buttresses which finish in pinnacles, its pair of stair turrets at the west end and, on the ridge, the bellcote for the sanctus bell, which was rung at important moments during the Mass.

Halsall Church gives the impression that an attempt was made, albeit in vain, to build the nave and chancel to one design. The earliest surviving church in Lancashire where this appears to have happened is at **Tunstall**,

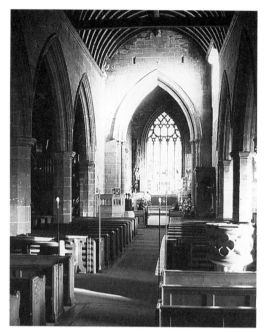

Halsall

up in the Lune Valley almost in Cumbria or North Yorkshire. **St. John's Church** now lies outside the village, in a graveyard full of yew trees, but it probably marks the approximate site of the original village which has subsequently moved towards the present main road. The church was rebuilt in about 1415 by Sir Thomas Tunstall of Thurland Castle, so it may be his effigy which lies in the south-east chapel. The church is not as imposing as the chancel at Halsall, but, when it was built with its sturdy tower and two-storey porch, it was grander than most other parish churches in the County. I find it immediately appealing in its sturdy simplicity and uniformity of style, which can be seen better on the north side than on the south, and better still inside, where the arcades run from east to west without a break.

There is, fortunately, little stained glass, so the church is light, although it has no clearstorey. The glass in the east window is of more than usual interest, however, since it comes from the Low Countries and was made four or five hundred years ago. The central panel, showing Christ giving the keys of the Kingdom of Heaven to St. Peter, dates from the sixteenth century, while the side panels with the Madonna and Child and St. Anthony are perhaps a century older. The right-hand side of the easternmost window of the north aisle has something even older – part of a Roman altar dedicated to Aesculapius, the god of medicine, and to Hygeia, the goddess of healing, by a man called Julius Saturninus. This was found in 1912 and probably came from the Roman fort whose remains lie under the ground near

Burrow Hall; but there are better examples in Lancaster City Museum.

To those with a love of English literature Tunstall Church is most interesting because it was the model for Brocklebridge Church in Charlotte Brontë's novel 'Jane Eyre'. She and her sisters were unhappy pupils at the Clergy Daughters' School founded in 1823 by the Vicar of Tunstall, the Reverend William Carus-Wilson. Every Sunday they had to walk from Cowan Bridge (where the School building still stands on the A65 just north of the bridge) and eat their packed lunch between the services in the room above the porch. This was reached in the late 1820s, not by a ladder, but from a gallery which stood at the west end of the church.

The finest medieval church in the County is **St. Mary's** in **Lancaster,** now known as the **Priory** because it stands on the site of Lancashire's first monastery. It looks particularly well when seen with the Castle from across the river, or from the south-east as one toils up the hill on which it stands. The only features of the present church which a medieval monk would certainly recognise are the main doorway, which dates from around 1200, and the mid-fourteenth-century

doorway which now leads from the church into the tower, but originally led outside because the old tower stood further north. The rest of the church was probably built about a century later, after the original monastic community had been disbanded by Henry V in 1413 during the Hundred Years' War with France. This is because it was what was called an 'alien priory', that is, one which was subordinate to an abbey in France and might, it was feared, send not merely money but information to the French. Not all, but many, alien priories were dissolved, as well as having their links abroad cut. In the case of Lancaster, the estates whose produce and rents had supported the priory were confiscated from the Abbot of Sées and given to Syon Abbey, which the King had recently founded near London. In return, the Abbey paid for the building of a new parish church, a little wider and at least half as high again as any other church nearby. The church's size must reflect the extent of the medieval parish of Lancaster, but the scale of the building is probably due to the self-esteem of Syon Abbey, which was doubtless encouraged by its royal patron, who was also the Duke of Lancaster, to provide a building which would reflect its status and importance.

Lancaster Priory

In this, I think, it succeeded. The church is faced almost all over with well-dressed stone and gives the impression of being built to a single design. All the windows in the aisles are similar in appearance, and it is only inside that one notices that the pillars and arches and the clearstorey windows beyond the chancel arch are more richly fashioned than those in the nave. One can see the joint between the richer and the simpler work in the north-east arch of the nave, and this shows that the nave was built after the chancel (as one would expect). This simpler design may have been an economy measure, but probably does no more than reflect a change in fifteenth-century taste.

As one comes into the church, one cannot fail to see the three fine Georgian chandeliers hanging from their newly gilded supports, and it is worth while searching out two or three of the eighteenth-century monuments in the aisles of the church, especially the elegant one in the north-east chapel to Sybill Wilson who died aged six years in 1773. Her grieving parents are represented in Roman dress, but this was not very unusual at the time. To the north of the north aisle stands the chapel built in 1903 to commemorate the officers and men of the King's Own Royal Regiment who had died in the Boer War. Hanging from its walls is one of the largest collection of regimental colours in the country. It also contains some of the four Coptic crosses which were rescued by the regiment during a war in Abyssinia in 1868. Nobody really knows how old they are but, if they do date, as is claimed, from the fifth century, their incised drawings of scenes from the Gospel stories must be among the oldest in existence.

The church's greatest treasure is its set of fourteen wooden choir stalls which were carved about 1345. There are only two or three older sets in England, and these stalls in Lancaster are regarded by experts as an outstanding example of English carpentry skills and a real masterpiece of the carver's art. So important are they that two were prominently displayed at the Royal Academy's 1987 Winter Exhibition on Art in Plantagenet England and were described in the catalogue as 'without doubt the most spectacular woodwork monument in the exhibition'. Each stall has a magnificent canopy, sumptuously carved with leaves set around and above flamboyant traceried panels, each different from its neighbour and

separated from it by a richly crocketed pinnacle. There are at least a hundred little heads and faces carved among the panels. Ten of the stalls have their misericords, which are not as interesting as those at Whalley, and all of them are decorated with attractive tapestry backs and cushions, whose motifs emphasise the links between the church and the local community. These embroideries were worked by women of the parish between 1962 and 1975.

The tower of Lancaster Priory is not medieval; it was in fact finished in 1755 and must therefore be regarded as the earliest building of the Gothic Revival in the County — of which more later in Chapter 7. At most of the medieval churches in Lancashire, however, a late-medieval west tower is the finest feature. Almost every church I have mentioned so far has one, and most of them are remarkably similar in their design — with a three-light window over the west door, a plain storey (perhaps now with a clock) fronting the ringers' chamber and three-light bell-openings above, diagonal buttresses at the western corners and — more often than not — a staircase in a square projection at either of the eastern angles. With about three dozen to choose from, I find it impossible to have a favourite, though Broughton and Goosnargh come towards the top of my list, closely followed by the sixteenth-century towers at St. Michael's-on-Wyre and at Ormskirk. The latter was built to house the bells from Burscough Priory and makes a strange partner for the church's earlier octagonal steeple, which is like the one at Halsall.

Lancaster Priory — Choir Stalls

26

Ormskirk

The **parish church of St. Peter and St. Paul, Ormskirk,** is quite stately, but I always find it a little disappointing, perhaps because it is largely a Victorian rebuild; but the south-east chapel contains four interesting sixteenth−century effigies. They are said to be those of the first Earl of Derby and his two wives − the second one being Lady Margaret Beaufort, the mother of Henry VII − and of the third Earl, whose son had the chapel built between 1574 and 1579. In the Scarisbrick Chapel, which precedes the Derby Chapel, there is a very fine brass figure on the south wall − a little difficult to see between two large windows − commemorating Sir Henry de Scarisbrick who was knighted after the battle of Agincourt and returned later to fight in France, where he died in 1420. Like the Derby monuments, this one must have come from Burscough Priory.

The two finest medieval towers in the County are unlike any of the others and stand at Bolton-by-Bowland and at Hornby, the first set between two greens in a pretty, well-treed village in a part of Lancashire which used to be Yorkshire before 1974, and the second in the heart of the Lune Valley.

The **Church of St. Peter and St. Paul** at **Bolton-by-Bowland** was built in the mid-fifteenth century. It is typical of many churches in the Craven area by being fairly long and somewhat low, but its aspiring tower, which was rebuilt to the original design in 1852, counterbalances this very well. It is unusual − but this contributes to success of the design − in having bell-openings in both of the stages above the roof of the nave; what is more, they are linked by a slightly projecting mullion which rises from the head of the lower opening and across the upper one right to the battlements of the roof.

Bolton-by-Bowland

After such splendour the interior is disappointingly squat in its proportions, but it contains a set of seventeenth-century pews, a rather fine early sixteenth-century font with a concave-sided octagonal bowl decorated with the coats of arms of local gentry families, and a grave-cover the like of which I have never seen. It lies on a Victorian tomb-chest under the arch leading to the Pudsay chapel (south of the altar) and commemorates Sir Ralph Pudsay, his three wives and their children, all of whom are represented in three rows of small figures beneath the much taller figures of their parents. In the lower folds of her gown each wife has the Roman numeral indicating the number of children she bore: six, two and seventeen, making a grand total of twenty-five. The art-historical interest of this monument — as distinct from its considerable human interest — is that, though it is made of the local limestone, the figures are represented by incised lines, as though it were a brass memorial like the one to Sir Henry de Scarisbrick at Ormskirk.

The tower at Bolton-by-Bowland is more stately than the one at **St. Margaret's Church, Hornby** but I find the latter more attractive, though perhaps because it is more unusual. It was built in 1514, as its prominent Latin inscription over the west window states, by Sir Edward Stanley, the first Lord Mounteagle. He was a junior member of the great Lancashire family and had led the Lancashire contingent at the battle of Flodden Field in 1513. For his part in the crushing English victory — which we now know gave more than a century of peace to the North West because no Scots army was seen in Lancashire until 1648, during the

second part of the Civil War — he was rewarded by Henry VIII with a title and some estates. The tower is remarkable for being octagonal and, furthermore, for the way in which the upper parts are twisted relative to the lower ones, though this created problems about the tidy disposition of the niche and the coat of arms.

Lord Mounteagle also had the chancel built, though he died in 1524 before it was complete, and it too is unusual. It complements the tower by being semi-octagonal in plan, with the result that its east window is placed between two smaller ones set at an angle, a feature which is as graceful inside as out. Grace is in fact the key-note of the interior, which was rebuilt in 1889 with arcades and a clearstorey placed between early nineteenth-century walls in a design of great distinction and discretion by the Lancaster architects, Paley and Austin, of whom I shall have more to say in Chapter 7.

But, before looking ahead too far, let us look backwards once more. Outside the south wall of Hornby Church is the tall base of an Anglo-Saxon cross carved with arches in low relief rather like the ones at Heysham. Inside the tower of the church there are several more fragments of pre-Conquest crosses, including one which is carved with two figures under a tree with loaves and fishes at their feet. We started with ambiguities and apparent hesitation at Halton and now finish with a scene whose Christian symbolism is beyond doubt. Perhaps the Normans were wrong after all to regard their conquest as also a crusade.

Hornby

Chapter Three
Traditional Houses

Gawthorpe Hall

3. TRADITIONAL HOUSES

Many people come to Warton near Carnforth to see a stone inside the north-west corner of the tower of the parish church which is carved with the original Stars and Stripes — the arms of the Washington family who lived at Warton for about two hundred years before 1530. But, to my mind, a more interesting relic of past glories lies on the other side of the road. This is the building now called the Old Rectory which stands behind the present vicarage. It is a roofless shell — a ruin, to put it more bluntly. I must admit that I prefer old buildings which are well maintained and furnished, but ruins can, on occasion, be of considerable interest because they enable us to see the basics behind the wallpaper, in the same way as a skeleton reveals the underlying structure of the human body.

which were probably storerooms for food and drink — known technically as the pantry and the buttery. They had above them a room, a chamber with a fireplace, which would have given the owner and his family a degree of privacy from the rest of the many inhabitants of the house.

The tall room on the right, which was originally open to the steeply pitched rafters of the now non-existent roof, was known as the hall and was the centre of everyone's life — not merely a communal living room for the lord of the manor's family and servants, and a court of law on occasion, but also the administrative headquarters of the manor (or landed estate) whose produce paid for the house to be built and maintained. There is no sign of a fireplace in the walls, so the room

Warton Old Rectory

What the **Warton Old Rectory** displays is the standard plan and cross-section of a medieval manor house, the germ from which all the splendours of the English country house were to develop. All the main windows have gone except for one in the right-hand gable, but that, along with the mouldings on the doorway arches, shows that the building probably dates from the early fourteenth century. As one enters through the present front door, one notices that there is a back door immediately in front at the end of what is called the cross passage; to one's left are three identical doorways, of which the central one leads through a corridor to the outside kitchen — outside to reduce the risk of fires. The other doorways lead to rooms,

must have been heated by a fire on an open hearth in the middle of the floor; this was the normal practice in the fourteenth century, even in the houses of the gentry. The smoke would have found its way out as best it could through holes in the thatch, but there may well have been a sort of wooden chimney, called a louvre, built between the rafters.

By our standards, with draughts from the front and back doors and perhaps from unglazed windows, and with a somewhat smokey atmosphere, this would not have been a comfortable room, but by the standards of most medieval Lancastrians it was luxurious. Second only to a large retinue of servants and men-at-arms, a fine hall was

31

the ultimate status symbol in the Middle Ages, so much so that even today the word Hall is taken to mean the most important house in a village. This hall in Warton was designed to impress visitors with the wealth and importance of its owner, and it would have done so. For a start, it was built of stone — limestone rubble for the walls and sandstone (which is easier to carve) for the doorways and windows — whereas most people lived in houses with wooden frames. It was spacious and, above all, it was tall. This all meant that it was expensive.

The house would not have been fitted out to anything like our modern standards. In the lord's first-floor chamber — which was, basically, a bed-sitting room where close friends or particularly important guests could be received — the walls might have been hung with tapestries and the floor would have been of timber boards, rather than of rammed earth under layers of rushes; there would have been a double bed with curtains, a chest or two for clothes and precious possessions, and a few stools. The hall would have been much more sparsely furnished, because it was an all-purpose room.

The tables there were boards on trestles, and they and the benches would have been ranged flat around the side walls except at meal times to clear as much space as possible around the potentially dangerous open hearth. At meal times retainers sat at tables along the side walls, while the lord and his family and guests sat at a table on a slightly raised dais at what was called the upper end of the hall, away from the draughts of the cross passage. By the fourteenth century the tendency was growing (at least in the South and Midlands) for the lord of the manor to eat most of his meals in his chamber, and only to eat in the hall on particularly important occasions; by about 1500 such a practice was also common in the North and a source of concern to contemporary moralists who saw it — rightly — as a sign of the break-up of the traditional society (which we call 'feudal'). The same thing had happened in monasteries, where the abbot, who had originally lived with his monks, was having special lodgings built, where he too might discuss matters confidential and also enjoy the pleasure of privacy.

Who was the builder of this house at Warton? Nobody knows. It is called the Old Rectory because the tradition says that it was built by the rector of the parish, who was not necessarily a priest. The fact that the building stands behind the present vicarage, across the road from the church, lends some credibility to this story but cannot be regarded as proof.

A few paragraphs ago I implied that Warton Old Rectory was exceptional because it was a medieval house built of stone. The most common building material until the seventeenth century was, undoubtedly, timber — even though very few timber-framed buildings survive in the County. Two of the finest which do are Samlesbury Hall and Rufford Old Hall, and both are well worth a visit.

Samlesbury Hall

There are those who claim that **Samlesbury Hall** was built in 1325, but there is little evidence for this except hope, which springs eternal in the amateur historian's breast, or that curious snobbery which regards something older as something better. Regardless of its dates, Samlesbury Hall is certainly one of the most striking black and white houses in the North West and must have distracted many a driver on the Blackburn to Preston road. The most photogenic part is in fact not the oldest part; this is the hall, which is short and stands to the right of the big bay window. One can get a hint of what one will see inside through a little spy-hole in the right-hand gable, which gives a tantalising glimpse of a thick beam rising diagonally from left to right. Go inside the house, walk around to the right and you will find yourself in the hall; it is somewhat shorter than when originally built, but is endowed with two pairs of what are called cruck trusses.

Samlesbury Hall — Bay and Screen

A large amount of research in recent years has proved that crucks are not so rare and not always so old as used to be thought. There are several fine cruck barns in Lancashire which probably date from the sixteenth or seventeenth centuries, but crucks are now rare in houses — at least in houses built for the gentry. These crucks are therefore interesting and they are also undoubtedly impressive, rising up from the ground in a pointed sweep to the ridge, so that they (and not the walls) carry the weight of the roof. Two of the five trusses at Samlesbury are crucks, spanning about twenty-five feet from wall to wall and carrying an apparent cat's cradle of timber posts and braces above the cambered tie-beams. It is generally considered that they date from the early fifteenth century, a hundred years before the bay window and the screen, which stands next to it.

It is at this point that the hall at Samlesbury, for all that it contains some pleasing pieces of seventeenth-century furniture, becomes somewhat disappointing as a historical 'document', because one would not expect to find a screen and a bay window next to each other. Screens were sometimes placed between the cross passage and the hall in such a way as to reduce the draughts from the passage, which for this reason is often called the screens passage. What happened at Samlesbury during nineteenth-century 'restoration' work, was that the screen was moved from its original site at the **lower** end of the hall to stand by the newly-made entrance, even though that entailed placing it

by the bay window — the late-medieval status symbol par excellence which was invariably placed to light the lord's table at the **upper** end of the hall. The glass in the bay window dates from 1936 and represents the arms of ten kings and queens of England, but the mullions of the windows with their roll moulding suggest an early sixteenth-century date. The screen, as it now stands, is something of a hotch-potch of medieval and Jacobean woodwork, with an inscription dated 1523; above it, in front of what is wrongly called the minstrels' gallery, are three pinnacles, grotesquely carved like writhing monsters in a nightmare. There are similar pinnacles at Rufford Old Hall, but no-one knows where either set comes from.

The wing at right angles to the hall, and probably the square room above the bay window were built in the 1540s by Sir Thomas Southworth in the sort of timber-framing which came to supersede crucks in gentry houses by 1500 — although they were still used in poorer houses in the Fylde and the West Lancashire plain well into the seventeenth century. This sort of framing is called post and truss.

Without getting too technical, the problems with cruck construction are that builders needed heavy curved timbers (which were increasingly difficult to find) to form the paired crucks, and that there was no way of constructing a building higher or wider than what the available crucks would allow. Post and truss construction, on the other hand, used smaller pieces of (mostly) straight timber and was much more flexible: within reason, a building could be extended in depth, length, or even height, with relative ease. Perhaps the best example of this can be seen at Little Moreton Hall (which is in Cheshire not in Lancashire, but which everyone has seen on a calendar or chocolate box) where a whole storey was added in the 1570s to an existing building — to provide a fashionable long gallery. To be frank, the building would have collapsed before now, if wooden and, later, iron tie-bars had not been inserted — but my general point is not invalidated.

Post and truss construction involves building up a sort of square lattice of upright posts and horizontal rails pegged together to form front and back walls, which are linked at intervals to similarly framed cross-walls carrying triangular frames, called trusses, to support the roof. In the normally squarish space between the posts and rails a panel of wattle and daub infill was inserted, but in South Lancashire, as indeed in Cheshire, the local fashion was to strengthen these panels — not that this was really necessary — with four corner braces; sometimes these are merely straight but more often, as here at Samlesbury, they are specially shaped to provide a decorative motif of quatrefoils. It is generally thought that they were not originally painted black, and that such a striking contrast with the plastered infill is a Victorian innovation.

Sir Thomas' wing was probably built to contain family rooms, including a private parlour (which one sees first on entering) with a fireplace dated 1545 and a richly beamed ceiling. Beyond this is the chapel, and above these rooms is a fine long room — probably subdivided at first — which would have provided chambers. All of them had the now fashionable fireplace in the wall, and one of the chimneys outside carries the coat of arms of Sir Thomas, who wanted everyone to know who had built these striking examples of the latest status symbol. He built the wall between the stacks in brick because, after the dissolution of Whalley Abbey, he was able to buy a number of fine stone windows which could not easily be fitted into a timber-framed wall.

In later life Sir Thomas, who had been knighted while fighting in Scotland in 1547, was well-known, and punished, for his stubborn allegiance to Roman Catholicism; but he was a powerful and respected man in this part of Lancashire. He died in his bed and handed on his estates, hardly diminished, to his son and heir. It might seem strange to us that such a man should have been prepared to profit from the downfall of the Abbey, but the punishment meted out to the supporters of the Pilgrimage of Grace in 1536 would have encouraged a degree of caution, and he probably took the view that, if he did not buy the windows, someone else would. Doubtless, he was right, so we have him to thank, perhaps, for their survival.

Rufford Old Hall is the prettiest country house in Lancashire, set in a slightly wooded park between the Liverpool road and the canal and presenting a delightful contrast between medieval timber-framing and the mellow red brickwork of a wing added in 1662. A medieval doorway remains, with a pair of dragons carved in the lintel, but the main entrance is now through the brick wing. This houses on its upper floor part of an interesting folk museum which contains nineteenth-century costumes and West Lancashire bygones. It is worth spending some time there after visiting the great hall, which is my particular concern in this chapter.

Rufford Old Hall

Rufford Old Hall – Screen

The late-medieval hall, when one looks at it from outside, is obviously only part of the original building. In the gable wall to the right are two doorways which must have led to the private wing of the house; this probably had a gabled roof running at right angles to the main roof like the one on the left. If this had survived, the house would have provided a text-book example of the late-medieval gentry house with its hall and two cross-wings – one at the lower end for storage and service with a family room above it (as we saw at Warton) and one entirely for the family at the upper end, away from the noise and smells of the screens passage. On the ridge of the hall roof is a lantern, which was placed there in 1821 to remind people that there had originally been an open hearth here, while to the right is a fine bay window which shows that the Hesketh family were in the forefront of fashion in the late fifteenth century. It provides a good deal more light than the original windows which were all placed above the line of the doorhead (and may not have been glazed originally); it suggests too that the family felt reasonably secure.

One approaches the hall across, rather than through, the screens passage, but it is nonetheless impressive, being twenty-five feet wide, fifty feet long and nearly forty feet high. It is beyond question the finest medieval hall in the County and one of the best in the Kingdom. To reduce the draughts

from the main doors, the builders erected what is called a spere truss, with two enormous wooden pillars each carved out of a tree trunk and set about four feet inside the main walls to support a side screen. Between these pillars stands a richly panelled moveable screen – a relative term this, since the screen must literally weigh half a ton – with three outlandish twisted pinnacles, like those at Samlesbury, added later from Goodness knows where. On the other side of the passage are five doorways with decorated lintels which led originally to service rooms, a staircase and, perhaps, a separate parlour facing southwards.

At the further, or upper, end is the dais where the table for the lord and his family once stood; above it the ceiling was later coved to provide a sort of canopy to emphasise the importance of the lord of the manor. To the right is the tall bay window, added after the hall was built as a further status symbol. Above the coved ceiling of the dais a priest-hole was found during restoration work around 1900; it appeared to be genuine – unlike most cavities for which the claim is made – for the Heskeths were in Elizabethan times a Roman Catholic family. To the left is a sixteenth-century fireplace, half-filled inside and wholly rebuilt outside in 1821 when the windows on this side were greatly enlarged.

Rufford Old Hall – Upper End

The hall is decorated with an exuberance which – pleasingly – grows with the distance from the floor. Overall is the roof which is the principal glory of the house. It has no tie-beams spanning between the walls, but four pairs of projecting hammer beams with angels carrying shields and supporting arched braces which strengthen the principal rafters. In the centre of each truss, where the braces meet, there are big bosses carved with the coats of arms of the families with whom the Heskeths had intermarried. Within the roof itself are three tiers of windbraces – originally intended to stiffen the roof structure, but used here to form the largest decorative quatrefoils in the house, each with a centrepiece like a concave lozenge. I cannot help feeling that in this last detail the designer went too far.

It is sometimes possible to date a gentry building approximately from the heraldry incorporated in its design – provided, of course, that one knows the coats of arms of the local families. At Rufford, however, the two bosses nearest to the upper end break what appears to have been a sequence by displaying the badge of the Stanleys (the three legs of Man) and a Tudor rose. If I am right in supposing that there was a sequence, the fifth boss would have shown the arms of the Heskeths and the Massys of Rixton, which would suggest that the house was built around 1460 by Thomas Hesketh. Other people think that the house was built by his father, another Thomas, but no documentary evidence has yet come to light to prove the point either way. At this distance in time it does not matter much, perhaps, but what does interest me is that the Stanley badge also appears in the bay window which was definitely added to the original structure. To me this implies that the Heskeths were formally putting themselves under the protection of the most powerful family in the area – the Earls of Derby lived then at Lathom which is only five miles away – and were also publicly stressing their allegiance to the new Tudor dynasty. In the troubled times of the late fifteenth century just after what we know as the 'Wars of the Roses', if a little family pride had to suffer to ensure a higher degree of security, it was probably a price worth paying.

The next major house to survive in Lancashire was **Hoghton Tower** which was begun in the early 1560s. Standing proudly on its hill-top and looking for all the world like a small castle, it was an old-fashioned house, rather than an up-to-date one, when it was built by Sir Thomas Hoghton. But he was a fairly old-fashioned man, and a staunch Catholic who preferred to go into exile in Flanders in 1569 rather than live in Queen Elizabeth's Protestant England. He became a considerable benefactor of the English College which Cardinal Allen (who had been born at Rossall) founded at Douai. A large number of the sons of Lancashire's Catholic gentry were educated there during the next two centuries, including the Jesuit priests, Edmund Arrowsmith and John Southworth, who were executed in 1628 and 1654 respectively and now count among the recently canonised English Martyrs.

Hoghton Tower

Sir Thomas' house was built around a pair of courtyards approached under a gatehouse, just as though it had been built by a major nobleman a hundred years previously. It is undeniably impressive to drive up the long straight avenue from the main road and then walk up from the car park through the first gateway – even though the battlements may not be original – and to find oneself almost surrounded by hard gritstone buildings with mullioned windows. These were originally built as workshops, stables and lodgings for retainers and visitors, but some are now occupied by the de Hoghton family. Then up more steps, twice, and through another gateway – above which stood another tower which gave the house its name – and finally into the inner courtyard where the hall stands yet higher on the left. This looks, in its details both inside and outside, to date from the

Hoghton Tower – Courtyard

early seventeenth century and may well have been finished by Sir Thomas' nephew, Sir Richard, who was one of the first baronets to be created. There is little doubt that – in essence – one has seen much the same sights as James I saw, when he made his memorable visit here in the summer of 1617. A copy of the menu of the dinner served to him can be seen in the hall; but the chair in which he sat while he dubbed a loin of beef Sirloin – to the amusement no doubt of his assembled courtiers, but dismay of subsequent English-teachers who have to explain that this event does not give the origin of the word – is not at Hoghton but at Astley Hall.

You will have noticed that I have expressed slight doubt about the building's authenticity. It was damaged during a short siege in 1642 – among other incidents, the main tower blew up with the loss, it is said, of a hundred lives – and abandoned by the Hoghton family in the early eighteenth century, when they took up residence at the now-demolished Walton Hall. For nearly 150 years it was neglected, though later tenanted

by weavers and other craftsmen in the cotton trades; it was therefore spared from any Georgian rebuilding, but had to be substantially restored in the nineteenth century. It must be said, though, that the restoration work, begun in 1863 under the control of the Lancaster architect Edward Paley and completed in 1901 by R.D. Oliver of London, was very carefully done: the illusion is almost complete. The same is true inside: there is a fine staircase of the late seventeenth century and some attractive panelling made by nineteenth-century craftsmen working for the Lancaster firm of Gillow. There is also pleasing furniture and a fine collection of dolls' houses, while from the attractive gardens behind the house the splendid views seem to stretch over half the County.

Hoghton Tower appears now as a conscious attempt by an Elizabethan gentleman to give a new house an old-fashioned air, harking back to the times when the leading gentry could not be told by the monarch what to do, when they had bands of armed retainers to protect their interests and ensure that their will was done. A house at the opposite extreme is **Borwick Hall,** which shows the attempt of its owner Robert Bindloss to put behind him the defensive character of the house, which his father had bought, and to place a peaceful manorial façade of honey-coloured stone in front of the fortified pele tower which had stood there for a couple of hundred years. Robert Bindloss was the son of a Kendal cloth merchant who had made a small fortune selling and exporting Westmorland wool and had then bought an estate, so that he could style himself, and in time be regarded, as a gentleman. He is the first known example in this area of what one might unkindly call a nouveau riche gentleman — there will be more in the course of the next few chapters — but he was certainly not the first recorded instance.

Building a new house in front of an old pele tower cannot have been easy, and there are some awkward changes of level and sharp turns to negotiate when one visits the house. Basically, the lowest storey of the tower,

along with a back wing, were used as service rooms — there is a fine kitchen fireplace with an archway which is twelve feet wide — while the new wing, with its tall windows subdivided by horizontal transoms as well as vertical mullions, accommodated the hall and the private rooms which the family required. These were now becoming more numerous. I have already mentioned the late-medieval custom of the lord and his family eating in the chamber on the first floor. By Elizabethan times this 'great chamber' was definitely regarded as the most important room in the house, and the hall had declined in status. No longer (at least in new buildings) was it open to the roof timbers; instead it was given a ceiling so that a room could occupy the space above it and, consequently, make it possible to move from one wing to the other on the upper floor without having to come downstairs.

On the ground floor beyond the hall was the traditional parlour for the family's daily living, while the rooms on the first floor now included a withdrawing room (into which they could retire from the newly public

Borwick Hall

domain of the once private great chamber) and also bedrooms, because the chamber was by then seldom used as such for sleeping: the name remained, but the function had changed. Borwick declined from a gentry house to be a tenanted farmhouse in the eighteenth century. Much of the old panelling and furniture was therefore introduced at the beginning of this century when the house was carefully restored, but the plan and section of the original house can still be seen, with the great chamber over the hall and a withdrawing room over the parlour.

Probably the most interesting internal feature is the stone staircase, which is no longer a spiral in the normal medieval fashion, but is built in short straight flights around a central core. When a room on the first floor became the most important in the house, a more imposing staircase became necessary to serve as a worthy means of access; but the most interesting feature of this staircase would only have been seen by people who went up another storey. The top of the central core is crowned by a balustrade of approximately Classical columns bearing a slab, of which two of the edges are carved with the name ALIXANDER BRINSMEAD, MASON 1595. I know of no other comparable example: Robert Bindloss must have been very pleased with Borwick Hall to allow Brinsmead to 'sign' his work in this way.

Turton Tower

Another pele tower transformed was **Turton Tower,** which was converted and extended in around 1596 by its owner

William Orrell, whose son mortgaged and later sold the estate to the famous Manchester merchant, Humphrey Chetham. At Borwick, to the best of my knowledge, the original floors of the tower were kept, since it provided little more than service accommodation. At Turton, on the other hand, it is clear that the older floors were stripped out and that two storeys were built into the space originally occupied by three, before the tower was raised in better quality masonry to provide a new third floor. One can see traces of small blocked windows below the projecting string-course which runs around the building between the older and the newer work. These new rooms in the tower were state rooms – probably the hall on the ground floor with the great chamber above – and the service rooms were accommodated in a cruck-framed wing built to the north and now hidden behind nineteenth-century additions, which are more pretty than authentic.

These additions were the work of James Kay, a prosperous local cotton spinner who had long cherished the ambition of being Lord of the Manor of Turton and of restoring the Tower to its former glory. He bought the estate in 1835 from the descendants of Humphrey Chetham, who had leased it for several generations to a succession of tenant farmers. Much of what one now sees in the house is Kay's work: the window sills were lowered in the tower, the north wing was part-clad in stonework with curving Jacobean gables and later part-raised by another storey of apparent timber framing; and the staircase tower was widened. It has long been fashionable to decry the work of Victorian restorers, but it must be said that without their efforts, which often did involve gilding the lily, there would not be so many lilies for us to enjoy today. One of the buildings at Turton which will give twentieth-century restorers an opportunity to show their allegedly greater skill and discretion is the attractive gabled building which stands a hundred yards to the east. This must have been built in the early seventeenth century as a summer house, or to give good views over the surrounding landscape.

The interior of Turton Tower is largely a confection of the 1840s, especially the Morning Room which James Kay created to provide a snug panelled parlour. But much of his work used old materials like the original staircase balustrade, the seventeenth-century panelling in the Drawing Room, and the early eighteenth-century panelling in the Dining Room which was salvaged from Middleton Hall when that was demolished in 1848. The Tower contains a museum (now administered by the County Council) which contains some attractive pieces of seventeenth-century furniture, armour and weapons, and an enormous, ugly four-poster bed which dates in part from 1593. It was bought a hundred years ago by the Victoria and Albert Museum as a genuine Elizabethan piece, but is now known to have been restored and more lavishly carved in Victorian times.

The best example in Lancashire of an Elizabethan house over-restored in a flush of Victorian enthusiasm for the Good Old Days of Merrie Englande is **GAWTHORPE HALL** near Padiham, which the National Trust has recently refurbished to stress its Victorian, rather than its Elizabethan, character. This bold decision is something which I wholly applaud, since the Trust owns several fairly unchanged houses from around 1600 but none (I believe) where Victorian Romantic antiquarianism is so clearly felt.

It used to be thought — and the Kay-Shuttleworths who had the house remodelled between 1850 and 1852 were convinced of this — that Gawthorpe Hall was built around a medieval pele tower, as Borwick and Turton had been. I find this difficult to accept: the original building accounts survive in full — the oldest, I think, in the County — and make no mention of earlier work. Furthermore, it is known that in the original arrangement of the house there were no fireplaces in the outer walls and that all the flues rose within the centre of the building to form a fine display of chimneys above a not-quite central tower-room which was probably used (like the summer house at Turton) as a viewing platform.

It is clear, when one looks at the front of Gawthorpe Hall, that it is a building in which the older traditions are giving way to new tastes. The big mullioned and transomed windows are still there, and so are the bay windows, but the main (south) façade and also the one to the west (or left) are symmetrical, and — most noticeably — the house is tall and compact rather than low and spreading. If one looks at the plan and section, one will see that there are further changes. No longer is there a central hall with a service

wing to one side and a family wing on the other; instead, most of the service rooms are in the basement. This is hardly visible at the front but, because of the way the land slopes quickly down to the River Calder, can clearly be seen at the back. What is more, the hall is not an entrance hall as was traditionally the case, but stands in the back right-hand corner of the building. The original family dining room (called since the mid-nineteenth century the Drawing Room) is on the left of the front door and vestibule, and the great chamber may have been above it, though it was subdivided into bedrooms in the eighteenth century. Over them all, and running the whole length of the top floor, is the long gallery, the first example of this major status symbol of the generation on either side of 1600 to survive in the County.

The building accounts show that the foundation stone was laid on 27 August 1600 and that the carcase of the house was completed and roofed in June 1603, after which the fitting out took another two or three years. The master mason was called Anthony Whytehead, but nobody knows who the designer was. The question is, however, inappropriate because in the early seventeenth century there was no such person as an architect. The basic plan of a house (called then a 'platt') was worked out before building work began, but it and the detailed appearance of the building were often modified, as the work progressed and as the master mason after discussion with the owner felt best. The details of the interior decoration were thereafter similarly worked out by the owner and the joiners and plasterers whom he employed.

That said, there is sufficient similarity between the stark symmetrical design of the tall main façade and the unconventional, experimental nature of the plan at Gawthorpe and those of such famous houses as Longleat in Wiltshire and Barlborough and Hardwick Halls in Derbyshire to suggest that Robert Smythson, who was closely involved in their design, also had a hand in the design of Gawthorpe. Clearly an original mind was at work, and the builder of the house, the Reverend Lawrence Shuttleworth, was acquainted with people for whom Smythson had already worked. Shuttleworth was the rector of Whichford (near Banbury) and inherited the estate of Gawthorpe, plus others at Barton near Preston and Barbon near Kirkby Lonsdale, on the death of his

Gawthorpe Hall
— Drawing Room Frieze

elder brother; their father had made a fortune as a lawyer in London and had shrewdly invested it in land.

The Shuttleworths left Gawthorpe at the end of the seventeenth century, preferring Barton or London, but Robert Shuttleworth moved back in 1816, though he died fairly soon afterwards. His daughter and heiress Janet loved the house and in 1842 married a man, Dr. James Kay, who was prepared to move there and hyphenate his surname to hers. He had been a doctor in Manchester, where he had been so appalled by the ignorance of his patients that he campaigned successfully for government involvement in primary education and, on his retirement in 1849, earned a baronetcy for his endeavours. He and Lady Janet Kay-Shuttleworth called upon the architect Sir Charles Barry, then working on the new Houses of Parliament as well as several country houses, to refurbish their house. It was Barry or, more likely, a member of his staff who also designed some of the terraces of houses in the centre of Padiham which make the town more attractive than most of its neighbours.

Many changes — improvements — were made to the old house, but it is still possible to get a good idea in two or three of the rooms of what it was like when originally built. The least changed room lies to the left of the entrance and, though it was originally the family dining room, is now called the Drawing Room and is newly re-furnished in the mid-Victorian manner. Nevertheless, the panelling is such as one would expect from the beginning of the seventeenth century with square panels, enriched with little arches and high-quality marquetry of stylised foliage with the Shuttleworth coat of arms above the fireplace. Above the panelling is a delightful plaster frieze with a running trail of stems and leaves inhabited by a variety of little birds and animals, heraldic beasts, mermaids, and men and women in contemporary costume. Overall is a fine plaster ceiling with flat ribs, pendants and panels containing vine-trails and bunches of grapes — an obvious reference to one of the pleasures of the dining table.

The long gallery on the top floor, a place for indoor recreation in poor weather, is also fairly unchanged. It has a similar but less ornate ceiling and a chimney piece with the arms of James I above a fireplace decorated with lovely de Morgan tiles representing sprays of leaves and sailing ships. The chimney piece also contains inscriptions in Latin and English to remind young Shuttleworths that they should honour the King, fear God who controlled men's destinies, do good and seek peace — as James I did try to do. Family portraits were often hung in long galleries to remind the up-and-coming generation of the qualities they should emulate. The best example is at Towneley Hall where the long gallery was built in the 1620s; unfortunately, the portraits have gone, but the frames with their titles and implicit exhortations remain. At Gawthorpe there is now a fine collection of portraits (on loan from the National Portrait Gallery) of prominent people connected with politics and the arts in the later seventeenth century. They hang in front of a very boldly patterned wallpaper designed by Augustus Pugin.

What is now called the Dining Room (it was originally the hall) is very largely a Victorian room, though the screens passage with a gallery above it — which could have been used by minstrels — is at least in part Jacobean. The centrepiece of the room is the fireplace with its Minton tiles and its chimney piece carried on 'Doric' columns and carved

with the various coats of arms of the Shuttleworth family during the centuries and the contemporary initials K-S. The fine wooden stair, reached through a solidly built stone screen, was also designed by Barry in a vaguely Elizabethan style. It leads to the top floor, from where another staircase (not open to the public) leads to two more storeys of servants' rooms in the tower; this was raised by Barry, doubtless to emphasise his belief that the house had originally been a pele tower. Its parapet is inscribed with the Shuttleworths' traditional motto 'Justitia et Prudentia', which is more understandable than the other inscription which appears there and elsewhere in the house: KYND KYNN KNAWNE KEPE. I assume that this pseudo-medieval English, which goes with the Romantic remodelling of the house, means something like 'relatives should stick together' or 'blood is thicker than water'.

Gawthorpe Hall is a house of major art-historical significance with its compact plan and symmetrical façades; its long gallery is the earliest in the County, and the so-called Drawing Room the finest of its date in Lancashire. But what causes me to place it in my highest category is the remarkable

Gawthorpe Hall — Long Gallery

Just before the completion of the structure of the original house, work was begun on the great aisled barn to accommodate both oxen and corn. The masonry work was done by William and John Whitehead, who may have been related to the mason in charge of the house, and was completed in August 1604. The building of the timber frame for the roof was probably finished somewhat later, and it is a masterpiece of the carpenter's craft. There are now no more than a handful of such barns in the County, and this must be the finest — a wooden cathedral measuring some sixty feet by forty feet and raising its ridge on carefully jointed aisle posts, tie beams and rafters to a height of nearly thirty feet from the ground.

Lawrence Shuttleworth created a fashion when he built Gawthorpe Hall in the early years of the seventeenth century. Within a generation, though not one of the dates of building is known for sure, several other similar houses had been built in South Lancashire. A mid-eighteenth century painting of Haigh Hall near Wigan shows that, before its demolition in the 1830s, it had three storeys and two (or, more probably, three) tall bay windows on the front. Hall o' th' Hill has stood on its hill in Heath Charnock since 1724, but was built a century before on another site; it has three storeys, a central doorway, and a bay window at either end. But the best preserved of all these other houses modelled on Gawthorpe is Astley Hall at Chorley.

An early eighteenth-century painting of **Astley Hall** shows that it was built of brick with stone dressings and, as such, looked more immediately attractive than now in its present dress of 'Roman' cement, probably put on in the late eighteenth century. Both when it was built and also now, its most arresting feature is the vast expanse of windows in relation to the walls which support them. There is probably even 'more glass than wall' than at Hardwick Hall — a virtually unbroken screen of windows running right across the façade of the south wing. That it is in fact a screen can be seen if one walks around to the side, where the wings are lower. But a screen in front of what, and why is it no more than approximately symmetrical?

The building history of Astley Hall is more complicated than that of most of the major gentry houses in Lancashire and not fully

Gawthorpe Hall — Barn

collection of needlework, lace and costumes made by the last occupant, Miss Rachel Kay-Shuttleworth, who died in 1967. She had a life-long interest both in textiles and the crafts used to make them; she was also a very good needlewoman, as can be seen in the beautiful hangings and counterpane which she embroidered during the First World War for a bed now in the Huntroyde Room, the former best bedchamber on the second floor. To an ordinary visitor like me the displays of embroidered and woven fabrics present objects of great beauty and interest to be enjoyed; for a specialist they are but the tip of an iceberg because they are backed up by an immense reserve collection and library, which can be studied by appointment.

understood or firmly dated. The economic history of country house building has yet to be written, but I am inclined to believe that, in times when even more than today a family's major status symbol was its house, extensions and rebuildings were linked with the marriage of the son and heir to a woman with a good dowry. Marriage among the families of the gentry and nobility was, until well into the eighteenth century, much more a question of finance and local politics than of the affections of the young people concerned, and there must have been many cases where a rebuilding was a condition of a marriage settlement, as a wealthy father sought to ensure that his daughter would be provided with a standard of life and accommodation which squared with his pretensions.

The oldest portions of Astley Hall seem to be the west wing, that is, on the left behind the south front, and the north wing. Their timber-framed construction suggests that they were built in the late sixteenth century around a courtyard, which apparently had its main entrance on the north and hence its hall in the southern wing. This could tie in with the marriage in 1574 of Robert Charnock to Isobel Norris of Speke Hall near Liverpool. The east wing, as it is now, appears to have been rebuilt during the 1820s (probably by a member of the de Hoghton family). I wrote 'rebuilt' because the south façade is asymmetrical at just this point, which suggests that it was built to screen a building which was there already. But when? More ink has been spilt about this south wing than about any other part of the house.

There are clear indications in the roof of the west wing that it continued further to the south than it does now, and there is inconclusive evidence that there was a tall, independently-constructed, timber-framed building where the present hall now stands; but whether it was built after or before 1574 is not sure. My surmise is that the previous hall at Astley was a late-medieval building with an open roof such as we saw at Rufford, that it was left unchanged in the Elizabethan rebuilding of the north and west wings, but that it and the gables of its neighbouring wings were refronted in the 1620s. This would be fairly early in the lordship of Thomas Charnock who was married to Bridget Molyneux, a minor member of a family which in South Lancashire was second only in its power and influence to the Stanleys. A date of around 1625 would fit quite well with much of the decoration of the

Hall, both outside in its attempted symmetry with the pair of bay windows flanking the coupled 'Ionic' columns of the doorway, and inside where a good deal of panelling and plasterwork of that approximate date survives.

Astley Hall

The most notable features of the south wing are, of course, the two-storey hall – I shall return to its ceiling in the next chapter – the overmantel of its fireplace which most scholars believe to date from the early seventeenth century, and the series of painted panels set within arch-headed frames and representing all manner of 'heroes'. Whether or not they are in their original position is less interesting than the men and women whom they portray. Some like Queen Elizabeth and Sir Francis Drake, Henry IV of France and William the Silent of Holland are portraits such as one might have found then in many English Protestant households; but how does one explain Philip II of Spain, who launched the Armada, or Ambrogio Spinola, the Spanish general who sought to defeat the Dutch Protestants? Christopher Columbus and Ferdinand Magellan are perhaps not surprising at a time when Miles Standish (who may have been a local man) was establishing the Pilgrim Fathers in America, but what is one to make of Islamic soldiers like Tamerlane, Bajazet I, and Mohammed II who captured Constantinople? It would be fascinating to know who commissioned these pictures, for he must have been a man more broadminded than most of his, or our, contemporaries. I can only surmise that this unknown Jacobean

Astley Hall – Hall

gentleman was a soldier, such as a man today who could have photographs in his study of both Rommel and Montgomery, because he admires them both as professionals.

The most remarkable of the early seventeenth-century rooms in the house is the long gallery which runs the full length of the top floor with an unbroken expanse of windows on the west, south and east sides. Such rooms were designed for indoor exercise in poor weather, though in fine weather, of course, people could just sit in the sunlit warmth of a bay window to enjoy a good book, some needlework or a quiet conversation. Entertainment of a more boisterous but also skilful kind was provided by the shuffleboard table which must have been built in the room. The object of the game was like that in shove-ha'penny — to push a flat weight to within a hair's breadth of the table-end to score the maximum number of points. It must have demanded both strength and skill because the table, on twenty turned legs, is nearly twenty-four feet long.

Astley Hall is Chorley's museum. As well as items of local interest, there is a good deal of seventeenth-century furniture — chairs and chests in most of the rooms, four-poster beds in the second-floor rooms in the west wing and a superb Elizabethan one, supposedly used by Oliver Cromwell in 1648, in the low-ceilinged Oak Room above the Drawing Room; it has massive turned posts standing on little architectural fancies to carry the heavily moulded canopy, and a bedhead with delicate inlaid work within elaborately carved frames. The author of a 1922 article in **Country Life** called it 'the finest specimen of its age which has escaped destruction' and concluded that Astley should become a place of pilgrimage for every lover of English oak. He was right — the Hall is badly under-rated.

The early eighteenth-century painting of Astley Hall, to which I referred earlier, shows in the background the sort of house with two gabled wings which was on the point of becoming old-fashioned when the Hall was refronted in a more or less symmetrical fashion under a flat balustrade. Gawthorpe Hall along with Astley and also its contemporary in Lancaster, now called the Judges' Lodgings — with its flat-fronted symmetry and approximately Classical doorcase — showed the way in which the houses of the major gentry would develop in the years after the Civil War: compact plans, height rather than breadth, symmetry and Classical details used with understanding, as I shall describe in the next chapter. However, at least until the Restoration, minor gentry continued to build in ways which were traditional to the locality — that is, in the vernacular tradition — and farmers were to do so until well into the eighteenth century.

No-one knows more about these developments in this County than Nigel Morgan and Jonathan Ratter, who recently used my office as a base from which to carry out a three-year survey of historic buildings for the Department of the Environment and who are now writing a book for Manchester University Press on the traditional housing of Lancashire. Until this appears, our understanding of the ways in which house types reflect social and economic conditions in the seventeenth and eighteenth centuries will be, at best, incomplete, and I foresee that I shall have some revision to do in this chapter, if a second edition of this book is required. However, as I said in the Introduction, my purpose is not to write a history of Lancashire's architecture, but to introduce you to what I believe are the most attractive, interesting and accessible old buildings in the County. Most of the houses which I shall mention in the last few pages of this chapter are in private ownership; they can be seen without discourtesy from public roads or footpaths, but are not open to the public.

One exception to this statement is the **Old Hall** at **Heysham** which is now a public house. This is a much less fashionable house than Gawthorpe. It was built in 1598 (according to a now illegible datestone) for an unknown family who were obviously not as wealthy as the Shuttleworths. They must have been gentry, however, for the house has many of the hallmarks associated with gentry status — plentiful fireplaces, as the ten chimneys show; high rooms, as the tall mullioned and transomed windows indicate; and attics which are high enough to accommodate people rather than stores and lumber. It is built to the standard Elizabethan pattern with cross-wings on either side of a hall, which has a fine fireplace and is no longer open to the roof; instead it is ceiled over to allow a room above it. And the house is not yet symmetrical: the hall is entered at the left-hand end, as can be seen by the position of the porch.

Heysham Old Hall

A house which combines a traditional appearance with a symmetrical façade is **Hacking Hall** which was built in 1607 by Thomas Walmesley, the younger son of a gentry family who became wealthy as a Judge on the Northern Circuit and bought an estate on one of the most attractive stretches of the Ribble just to the west of Whalley. His house, which overlooks the junction of the Calder and the Ribble, with Longridge Fell in the background, has no tall windows but does have generous attics and gables galore: on the cross-wings, on the dormer over the central bay, and on each of the turrets which rise in the angles between the hall and the cross-wings. On the ground floor of the right-hand turret is the front door which leads — following tradition — into one end of the hall; in the same position of the left-hand turret is the bay window of the hall. Strictly speaking, then, the main façade is not symmetrical, but one sees it as symmetrical from a distance; and the masses of the building, with the double recession of the front façade and projecting chimney breast at the back, are composed with an almost complete symmetry which is symptomatic of future trends.

It is dangerous to be categorical, but I think that the earliest vernacular house with a completely symmetrical front is **Carr House** near **Bretherton,** which dates from 1613. This symmetry is contrived by placing the gabled porch in the centre of the façade between two slightly projecting cross-wings, which must originally have had gables. The house is built of locally produced brick, with dressings of stone which was probably brought from Whittle-le-Woods — an early example of this use of two materials which became common in the western quarter of the County where stone outcrops very rarely. The most interesting feature of the house is the lintel over the porch which gives the date in the bottom right-hand corner — the result of an unplanned inscription par excellence — and relates that the house was built for John Stones by his brothers Thomas, a London haberdasher, and Andrew, a merchant in Amsterdam, 'of their own charges'. What story underlies this inscription? I do not know, but guess that John was the eldest son who farmed the family estate, while his younger brothers sought and made fortunes in trade.

Bretherton — Carr House (detail)

Bretherton — Carr House

The old medieval pattern with hall and gabled cross-wings continued even later into the seventeenth century. The timber-framed Buckshaw Hall, which stands in the ordnance factory near Chorley and is therefore not accessible to the public, bears a datestone of 1654, but I am somewhat sceptical about its significance. (One should never believe datestones implicitly; they are not always in their original position). The datestone of 1626 at the brick-built Peacock Hall, Leyland, looks authentic enough, though the windows have lost their mullions, and I can only think of one genuinely later example of a gentry house on the medieval model. This is **Shuttleworth Hall** between Altham and Hapton, which was built in 1639 by a gentry family, the Ashtons of Chadderton, on an outlying estate. The interior was gutted in 1892, but externally the Hall looks rather like a mirror image of Heysham Old Hall, the major exception being the mullioned windows in the two gables which are of a form then quite common in North East Lancashire, with three lights under an ogee-shaped head – a pattern which was often simplified to three lights with the middle one higher than the ones which flank it.

Gables were to persist for another couple of generations, presumably because they had associations with cross-wings and, therefore, with gentry status. Probably the latest example is at the **Lamb Working Men's Club** in **Barrowford** which was originally called Bank Hall. The main body of the house may well be older, but the gabled porch and cross-wing to the right were added in 1696 by Thomas and Grace Sutcliffe. They have a third tier of windows which suggest attics, though these must be too low to provide much useful accommodation. The windows in the gables of the dormers in the nearby White Bear Inn at Barrowford, which probably dates from 1667, are now blocked and may always have been intended for ornament rather than use – to hint that the builders, members of the Hargreaves family, were gentry rather than merely yeomen .

A third house in **Barrowford** is **Park Hall,** which now contains the interesting **Pendle Heritage Centre,** the local history museum and study centre; it looks rather similar to the previous two but has a more complicated history. It was built and extended during the seventeenth century by the Bannisters, a minor gentry family, of whom the miler Roger Bannister is a descendant; their history, and that of the house and other old buildings in the Pendle area – and, of course, the Pendle Witches – can be well studied in attractive displays in the house, which also has a couple of rooms furnished in traditional ways. Outside there is a charming walled garden planted in the eighteenth-century manner, a series of cruck trusses brought from a barn in Cliviger and a small agricultural museum in the barn; the toll house, which I shall mention in Chapter 6, is also part of the Centre and its collection.

Pendle Heritage Centre

Bolton Peel

One of the most attractive gabled houses in the County is **New Hall, Clayton-le-Dale,** which was built in 1665 by a member of the Talbot family, minor gentry whose badge of a hunting hound can be seen above the front door. It has three full storeys and is symmetrical with three gables to the front — the central one over the projecting porch. Many people will remember this house as an empty and increasingly derelict eyesore, but in the last year or so it has been lovingly restored by a young couple and is now once more a pleasing landmark on the south bank of the Ribble near Ribchester Bridge.

Many yeomen families had never been able to afford cross-wings in their houses. When they first began to build houses of materials which are sufficiently durable to have lasted down to our days, they were content with houses with two rooms on each floor; cooking was normally done on the fire which warmed the main room of the house, and its original position can often be guessed by the presence of a single small window, now known as a fire window, which gave light to the inglenook. An attractive and early example of such a house (though altered inside) is called **Dun Cow Rib Farmhouse** on **Halfpenny Lane, Whittingham.** It was built as early as 1616 by Adam Hoghton who must have been a member of the gentry because there is a coat of arms above the door, below the rib (supposedly from a ghostly giant cow) which gives the house its name. The Hoghtons enjoyed 'all mod. cons' too, because one can see, projecting from the right-hand gable wall, a pretty little first-floor privy.

Another gentry house, whose builder Thomas Lister proudly announced the fact in an inscription over the door in the gabled porch (which gives not merely the date of the house, 1635, but also the cost, £855) is now the **Ribblesdale Arms** in the centre of the attractive village of **Gisburn.** The windows on the ground and first floors were modernised, probably in the early nineteenth century, but the windows on the second floor — normally, as I have said, a sign of gentry status — are original and, with their stepped form which I mentioned a few paragraphs ago, typical of North East Lancashire. This sort of house, but with only two storeys, was a common pattern for much of the rest of the century for reasonably wealthy farmers. There is an attractive example, dating from 1654, at **Lower House Farm, Charnock Richard;** it stands close to an old quarry but is almost entirely built of brick — even the mullions of the upper windows. A somewhat similar and probably contemporary example in stone is **Bolton Peel** near **Bolton by Bowland.** Here the presence of fire windows and a large chimney stack well to the right of the porch suggests that the front door led into the main room away from the fireplace, whereas at Charnock Richard the chimney stack is in line with the porch and thus suggests that from the door one enters a lobby and goes into the main room through a door alongside the inglenook. I always look at the relative positions of front doors and chimney stacks, because it can help one make intelligent guesses about the original plan of a house without getting nearer to it than the garden gate.

49

New Hall, Clayton-le-Dale must have looked somewhat old fashioned when it was built, and I cannot think of a later house built with gables by a gentry family. By 1665 most families, even of minor gentry, were forcing their houses into the strait jacket of symmetry with a dining room and a parlour on either side of the front door; the gabled cross-wing, which had once been a status symbol to emphasise the fact that the family had a large parlour and an upstairs chamber, was now relegated to the rear to accommodate the kitchen and other service rooms. One of the best examples of this tendency is the **Manor House at Slyne,** which is dated 1681 above the highly ornamental lintel of its central door. On either side on the ground and first floors are two cross windows with a single mullion and transom, while the three attic windows are much lower but placed symmetrically.

Absolute symmetry was rare in farmhouses before the eighteenth century, when the gentry fashion of rear service wings began to be widely adopted. Nevertheless, many farmhouses were almost symmetrical, and certainly had a central doorway, from the middle of the seventeenth century. **Hawkshead Farm** in The Nook, a pretty corner of **Bolton-le-Sands,** is an early and impressive example dated 1665. It has three storeys, no gables and a central doorway, and one has to look fairly closely to notice that the fire windows on the left are not matched on the right.

An almost symmetrical house, similar to Hawkshead Farm but with only two storeys, stands on the other side of Lancaster at **Shepherd's Farm, Cockerham.** It dates from 1705 but is significantly smaller, although it is probably the largest farmhouse to survive from that time in that part of the County. The reason is likely to be the relative poverty of the acid and low-lying land near Cockerham Moss, compared with the sweeter soils on the low limestone hills north of Bolton-le-Sands. Houses of durable quality could only be built when farmers could afford to do so; before then they had to make do with cottages built on crucks which necessarily had only a single storey plus a loft. This can be well seen at **Lower Thurnham,** where a two-storey house dating from around 1700 is called **Tall Cottage;** to us it does not look particularly tall, but it stands next door to a cruck cottage, and a second look makes clear why, when it was new, it got its name.

The vernacular tradition, which was based originally on the masonry techniques used in gentry houses in the late Middle Ages, lasted in country areas well into the so-called Georgian period, in which all gentry houses and most of those built for 'the middling sort of people' (as the phrase then was) were designed in the Classical manner. The latest dated house I know with mullions in all its windows is New Hall, Entwistle, which was built in 1742 for John and Mary Brantwood. It has a central two-storey porch, but its windows are not symmetrical — to the left they have four lights but five to the right. By the time it was finished, houses in Lancaster like what are now the Ring o' Bells pub or the Conservative Club had been built with fine Classically detailed door cases. But the vernacular tradition persisted even further, beyond the completion date of Lytham Hall, the County's finest Georgian country house. If one travels by car between Lancaster and Preston on the A6, one can see on the east side of the road just north of Bilsborrow a house dated 1779 with sash windows and a pediment over the doorcase; if one travels by train, the same house — it is called Green Bank — is just to the west of the line, and one notices that, whatever the front may have, the back has a mullioned and transomed window to light the staircase. I know of no later example until vernacular features were consciously revived in the mid-nineteenth century.

Lower Thurnham — Tall Cottage

Chapter Four
Houses in the
Classical Tradition

Lytham Hall – Hall

4. HOUSES IN THE CLASSICAL TRADITION

No-one could by any stretch of the imagination call Hoghton Tower a Georgian house, as it glowers proudly and defensively on its hill-top site. And yet, immediately above the gateway through which one enters the lower courtyard, which is still medieval in its feel if not its fabric, is a small decorative plaque showing the initials TH and a man wrestling with a bull, all set within a framework made up of approximately Classical motifs — two pediments and a couple of tiny 'Ionic' columns. Whether the TH stands for the builder Thomas Hoghton (who went into exile in 1569) or for his grandson who was killed in a fracas at Lea Old Hall in 1589, the surround with its Classical details is probably the earliest piece of Renaissance decoration in a Lancashire building and thus, perhaps, the seed from which our Georgian architecture sprang. I am not too sure about the last assertion; one is on surer ground at Stonyhurst, where the decoration of the great gateway, begun by Sir Richard Shireburne in 1592, was probably modelled on the example at Burghley House (in Cambridgeshire), the home of Queen Elizabeth's great Minister.

Stonyhurst is not normally open to the public, since it is a Roman Catholic boarding school, but, fortunately, a minor road from Hurst Green forms the first part of the great entrance drive and, as it turns away to the left, brings one quite close to the front of the house. This was designed, rather as Hoghton Tower had been a generation earlier, around a courtyard with the hall (which is now,

appropriately, the school dining room) on the further side. None of this can be seen from the road, but the great gatehouse is unmistakable, an affirmation of the power of the Shireburnes and of Sir Richard's pride in his ancient lineage and his contemporary culture. The motif of a triumphal arch, which can be seen within the lowest storey, was fifteen hundred years old and therefore very up-to-date — a Roman motif and thus appropriate in an age when educated people were well-read in the Latin classics, looked back across a thousand years or so of 'Gothic darkness' which they called 'the middle age' and sought in their present to recreate something of the values and beauties of the Roman world.

Sir Thomas Hoghton seems to have used two pairs of colonnettes as a simple decorative device, probably without realising — because there were very few people in his England who did — that these Classical columns (which he would have called 'antick' columns) with their differently shaped heads or 'capitals' were part of a structural and decorative system with a considerable logic. Sir Richard Shireburne, on the other hand — building Stonyhurst a generation later and mixing in Court circles — must have known that the sturdy columns with plain capitals were called Doric, that the more slender columns with ringlets (called volutes) in their capitals were known as Ionic, while the columns whose capitals were decorated with acanthus leaves were called Corinthian. He will have known too that, whenever the

Stonyhurst

53

Romans had used them together - as one could see, for example, in the Colosseum – the Doric columns, because they looked stronger, had been used at the bottom to carry, as it were, the rest, with the more highly ornate Corinthians standing above the Ionics.

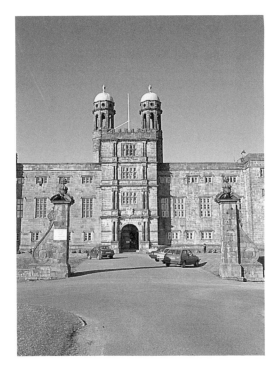

This is just what one sees on the gatehouse, with a fourth storey of even more highly decorated columns (called Composite) at the very top. What Sir Richard probably did not know – or perhaps he did not care – was that the Romans also had rules about the proportions between the height and diameter of the shafts of these columns, that Ionics were taller and slenderer than Dorics, and so on. While the lowest stage of the gatehouse is correctly proportioned and the details of the entablature (that is, the decorated stone beam carried by the columns) are accurately copied from Roman examples, the upper storeys of columns do not get taller – indeed, the opposite is the case. Although he and many gentlemen of his generation understood more about Roman architecture than their fathers had done, they still did not regard it as a system, but as a storehouse of decorative motifs from which they could take and use anything which caught their fancy.

Beneath this skin of appliquéd columns the gatehouse is basically a medieval building, and the windows in the walls on either side look little different from those of a hundred years previously; and yet by the end of the seventeenth century the builders of gentry

houses were to apply these Classical ornaments with an increasing understanding and a growing concern to be 'correct' by following Roman precedents.

The Shireburnes were the most important family in the Ribble Valley, but the Parkers of **Browsholme Hall** did not want to be left in the shade. When Thomas Parker was making alterations to his house in 1604 – probably to mark the fact that he had just bought the freehold from the King – he asked his mason, Thomas Holt, to provide a display of Classical columns; Holt did so, but with less understanding than the mason at Stonyhurst had shown. Others followed his example. At Gawthorpe Hall, which was being built at the same time, a single-storey doorway of approximately Classical form was applied – though it was changed by Barry in the 1850s. Thomas Covell's house in Lancaster (now the Judges' Lodgings) which was built in about 1620, had a version of a Doric doorway, while the doorway at Astley Hall is even more approximately Ionic.

Stonyhurst – Gatehouse

Browsholme Hall

The first surviving indication that the gentry of seventeenth-century Lancashire were aware of the work being produced by designers and craftsmen in Court circles is also at **Astley Hall.** Here, after the marriage in 1666 of Robert Charnock's heiress, Margaret, to Sir Peter Brooke of Mere in Cheshire, the entrance hall and the room to its right –

which is now called the Drawing Room, though it was probably a dining parlour — were redecorated in a slightly unsophisticated version of avant-garde design. As I wrote in the previous chapter, I surmise that the hall at Astley remained a two-storey room into the seventeenth century and was not subdivided horizontally when the new façade was given its grid of large windows in the 1620s. The painted panels and the carved wooden chimneypiece probably date from that time too, but what one notices immediately on entry into the hall is the plaster frieze and the ceiling above it — quite simply, because few people have seen anything comparable.

No building accounts or any other documentary evidence appear to survive, so one is forced back to the archaeological and heraldic evidence to estimate the date. The fact that there are cupids in the ceiling as well as the coats of arms of the Charnock and Brooke families in the frieze suggests that this decoration was carried out fairly soon after Margaret Charnock's marriage to Sir Peter Brooke; this would mean that the work is an early example in the North of England of a style of decoration introduced in London during the Commonwealth, and used

especially after the Restoration. There is no reason, as has often been suggested, to suppose that French or Italian craftsmen were involved. The lack of grace in the design, despite the skilful craftsmanship, suggests on the other hand that the work was done by a provincial craftsman who had seen such work in London or, more probably, was trying to copy what he had seen in an engraving.

The ceiling is divided into eight compartments, which correspond to the beams supporting the floor of the Long Gallery. Within these compartments there are alternately circles and ovals, richly decorated with twisted scrolls and wreaths of flowers and fruit, and surrounding either a rose or a cupid who is carrying his bow and arrow. One of the cupids was taken down for repairs in 1986, and I had the opportunity of looking at him closely. He was about two feet six inches long and weighed more than a child of the same size, for he was made of a wooden frame padded out with plaster and hessian and then moulded. The scroll around him was made of twisted leather — and so, I imagine are those along the beams — while his bow and arrow were made of lead then limewashed. The beams themselves are decorated with stylised acanthus leaves.

Astley Hall – Hall Ceiling

Below them is a two-feet-deep frieze with more scrolls and wreaths, the families' coats of arms and garlands of flowers, among which there are more cherubs playing ball and flying around. It is certainly a source of delight, if not quite a thing of beauty.

The whole room was designed to impress – as in the Middle Ages – and must have done so, when it was built, even more than it does today. The hall had lost its medieval status as the most important room in a gentry house in Elizabethan times, but after the middle of the seventeenth century its importance was growing once more. It was the first room seen by a visitor to a house and, as first impressions are important, it was increasingly designed to display the wealth and taste of the owner of the house.

The ceiling of the bay window in the hall is decorated with a sort of scallop shell from which a cherub swings like a mini-Tarzan. The ceiling of the Drawing Room, which attracts one's eyes completely away from the tapestry and the furniture, has more of these shells. It is lower and even more boldly moulded, though to a slightly different and, probably, slightly later pattern. There are no more rectangular compartments; instead only a great oval wreath with twisted scrolls and flowers within which are four shells and two cherubs holding onto garlands. Around this centrepiece are four roughly triangular corner pieces decorated with what I imagine are meant to be fronds of palm leaves, though they always remind me of fishes' ribcages! I imagine that they were made by someone who had seen a drawing of ceilings such as those at Sudbury Hall in Derbyshire, which are inventive and beautiful. These at Astley are not really a pretty sight but are certainly a tour de force of the plasterer's skill.

The balustrade of the fine staircase which rises to the left of the fireplace is also similar to the one at Sudbury. The newel posts are ornamented with what are called 'drops' of fruit and carry wooden vases filled with more fruit, while the balustrade is carved with rich scrolls of acanthus leaves and more cherubs. The risers are more richly decorated than usual, in that they have a curved profile. This staircase must have replaced a less ornate one – parts of whose balustrade remain on the upper floor – because a special compartment was built of brick to house it, as can be seen from the courtyard.

Astley Hall – Drawing Room Ceiling

The next remaining major architectural work in the grand manner which is open to the public is Towneley Hall near Burnley; but before we go there, I should just mention the work which was carried out at **Stonyhurst** by Sir Nicholas Shireburne, the last lord of the manor. Part of this work can be seen from the public road: it consists of the two octagonal turrets topped with domes and eagles, which Sir Nicholas had built to crown the gatehouse, and the gatepiers with open pediments and urns which were used to divide up the formal gardens, laid out around the house by James II's gardener, Henry Wise. All that one can see of these is the pair of 'canals' which flank the drive, but behind the house to the right are a pair of charming early Georgian pavilions at either end of a terrace which overlooks the Ribble Valley. (They can be seen at a distance from the public footpath to the east of the school). With their beautifully dressed stonework, garlands of stone flowers and roofs in the shape of concave pyramids they are the first buildings using Classical motifs which one can look at with pleasure as well as with interest.

Sir Nicholas died in 1717. His daughter Mary had married the eighth Duke of Norfolk and, after his death in 1732, returned to live at Stonyhurst. It was she who inserted the early fourteenth-century window from the family's long-demolished ancestral home, Bayley Hall, into the chapel where it can be seen to the right of the gatehouse. When she died in 1754 the estate and house passed to the Weld family of Lulworth in Dorset. They never lived here, but forty years later Thomas Weld, hearing that his old school, the English Academy at Liège, had been forced to close by the French Revolutionary army, offered the house and its grounds to the Jesuits to use as a school. They came, and Stonyhurst has been a school ever since.

If pleasure is the appropriate reaction to looking at the Stonyhurst pavilions, surprised admiration is the likely response towards the hall at **Towneley Hall.** From the outside the house is fairly dour, with a vaguely medieval appearance which owes more to the Romantic antiquarianism of several generations of later owners than to the Middle Ages themselves. One approaches the hall through an open courtyard which was surrounded until the mid-eighteenth century by buildings on all four sides. What one sees now represents basically the medieval hall and two extended cross-wings. Passing through the vaguely Gothic porch with its worn wooden door dated 1530, one suddenly finds oneself in the middle of the long side of a two-storey hall, lined out with tall fluted Ionic pilasters carrying an entablature, above which the attic storey and ceilings are richly decorated with elaborate plasterwork. This is without doubt the finest early eighteenth-century room in Lancashire, built for Richard Towneley soon after 1725 and decorated by the Italian plasterers Francesco Vassali and Martino Quadri who

Towneley Hall – Hall

were working in several houses in the North of England at that time. The original entrance to the hall was on the left where - outside - one can see a blocked doorway which used to lead to the screens passage, but by the eighteenth-century symmetry — and therefore a central door — was essential.

The builder's name is unknown and not important, for the character of the room depends so much on the quality of the plasterwork. Vassali and Quadri were doubtless chosen because they could turn a big space into an impressive space, suggestive of the power and cultural discernment of their patron. The modelling of the drops, of the foliage surrounds and of the arabesques in the ceiling (which Georgian craftsmen called 'frets') is in lower relief than at Astley but subtly emphasised by being picked out in cream on grey. In the coves between the attic windows there are playing cherubs, while medallions of Roman emperors hang between the pilasters. To the left, the fireplace has a richly scrolled overmantel which serves as a pedestal for a copy of the statue of the Medici Venus; the opposite fireplace carries the Dancing Faun. These were two of the favourite statues among eighteenth-century gentry, and copies of them can frequently be seen in Georgian country houses. The medallions of Roman emperors were meant to suggest — rightly — that Richard Towneley was a powerful man in the area and, just to make sure that no-one should leave without knowing to whom all this magnificence is due, his coat of arms with eighteen quarterings hangs proudly over the doorway. Since Vassali and Quadri's bill for the plasterwork at Towneley came to £185.11s.4d — only £25 more than the cost of the last Shireburne tomb a generation before — I imagine that Richard Towneley was quite satisfied.

Their bill included similar plasterwork on a new staircase to the left of the hall, which superseded an early seventeenth-century one to the right. It was built on the then relatively new principle of the cantilever, where each tread is built into the wall and also carried on the one below; since there are no newel posts, everything appears self-supporting and has an air of daring lightness as it climbs up around an open well. This lightness is emphasised by the balustrade, which does not have turned wooden balusters, but is made of excellent wrought-iron work said to be by Robert Bakewell, one of the most famous smiths of the early eighteenth century.

Gisburne Park — Staircase

Like Astley Hall, Towneley Hall is now a local museum and has some interesting exhibits to appeal to many tastes, from prehistoric flints to seventeenth-century furniture, a model of the brilliantly successful charge of the Heavy Brigade of cavalry led by a local soldier, General Sir James Scarlett, at the battle of Balaclava in 1854, plus some attractive water colours including some by Girtin, de Wint and Turner. I have already mentioned in chapter 2 the priests' vestments from Whalley Abbey, which are probably preserved here because the Towneleys were a Catholic family. A reminder of the sufferings of Catholics who would not take the easy way out by occasional appearance at the services of the Church of England is a portrait painted in about 1600 of John and Mary Towneley and their fourteen children, which also records the fines and imprisonments which John Towneley had to endure for maintaining a place of Catholic worship in this area. The chapel is no longer in its original position and now contains a splendid early sixteenth-century Flemish altar piece. This consists of six minutely carved scenes of the sufferings and crucifixion of Christ, set under traceried canopies of great delicacy; it was brought to the house by Charles Towneley, one of the most learned collectors in the eighteenth century. There is a portrait in the house of him, his dog and his friends among his famous collection of antique sculptures, which were bought after his death in 1805 by the British Museum.

There is plasterwork of comparable quality by Vassali and Quadri and a wrought-iron balustrade similar to the one at Towneley in the staircase at **Gisburne Park.** The plasterwork is, perhaps, even more interesting, because several of the panels are filled with bas-reliefs of incredibly delicate modelling — cherubs playing music in front of an Alpine landscape, and a young man drawing a scene which one can actually see on his paper — as well as more conventional frets and scrolls. Gisburne Park is now a private hospital and only occasionally open to the public, so the most lavish display of plasterwork from the 1730s which one can see easily is at the **Music Room** in **Lancaster.** This was a semi-derelict ruin until about a dozen years ago when it was rescued in the nick of time and restored by the Landmark Trust, whose architect Edward Mason cleverly contrived a holiday flat in the attic storey. It can now be seen across a courtyard laid out off Sun Street by the City Council.

It looks rather strangely out of place, with its pilastered façade surrounded by the backs of buildings of no great quality, but when it was built, it was a summer house in a garden belonging to a house on Church Street, which is now the Conservative Club. Inside, the room on the first floor (accessible by the door on the right) contains a very exuberant display of plasterwork — perhaps produced

by Vassali and Quadri, though much of the modelling of the figures is not so accomplished as the work known to be by them. Above the fireplace stands the god Apollo with his lyre, flanked by two Muses. On other walls are the other Muses with displays of musical instruments. In the ceiling is Ceres, the goddess of agriculture, surrounded by garlands of fruit and flowers and medallions bearing portraits of Roman emperors. I cannot help feeling that the decoration is too crowded, but readily accept that it is an impressive display of the plasterer's skill.

Decorative plasterwork of this quality was an expensive way of covering a wall, and skilled craftsmen were few and far between; it was therefore only commissioned by richer gentry. Less wealthy gentlemen had to content themselves with simple panelling which could be produced by any competent joiner. In better examples the work followed seventeenth-century precedents and was made of oak; in work of lesser quality pine wood was used and had to be painted to hide the knots and variations in the grain. A good example of better-quality Early Georgian panelling is to be found in the right-hand ground-floor room of the **Judges' Lodgings Museum** at **Lancaster,** which I have so far only mentioned in passing but which is well worth a visit. The panelling is typical of its date in being divided by tall fluted pilasters (of the Doric order), and the panels themselves are long and fairly narrow above

Lancaster — Music Room

the dado rail; they are also 'raised', that is they are slightly proud of the surrounding woodwork. The finest feature of the room, which is sparsely furnished as was normally the case in eighteenth-century houses, is the cupboard opposite the windows which has probably always been used to display porcelain. It is built in the form of a niche with a shell-shaped top and is painted in the grey-green paint often used at that time – since the pigments necessary to make the paler colours which we prefer were then very expensive.

thrice-yearly attendance at the Assizes. Some of the first-floor rooms are therefore furnished as they were when used as a bedroom, drawing room and dining room in early Victorian times by the visiting judges. Others contain an exhibition on the firm of Gillows, whose former works and shop (built in 1770) stand to the left of the Judges' Lodgings at the top of Church Street; needless to say, the exhibition not only displays the tools which traditional craftsmen used but also some fine pieces of the furniture which they produced during the century

Lancaster
– Judges' Lodgings (LCC Museums)

The Judges' Lodgings are the home of one of the most interesting museums in the County – really, three museums in one. The house was originally built around 1620 by Thomas Covell, the Constable of Lancaster Castle and then became the town house of a local gentry family whose estate was a few miles to the north. They sold it in 1826 to the County authorities and for nearly 150 years it accommodated the judges during their

from 1770 to 1870. Finally, on the top floor is the very popular Museum of Childhood. This has displays (which stimulate everyone's memories) on baby-care, on the development of dolls and toys from the eighteenth century until the present, plus rooms furnished as Edwardian day and night nurseries, and an Edwardian schoolroom where one can try to sit in the desks and write on the slates.

The finest Georgian house in the County is, beyond question, **LYTHAM HALL.** It was bought a few years ago and redecorated to its former splendour by the Guardian Royal Exchange assurance group, which arranges an occasional open day for the public. It was built between 1757 and 1764 to the designs of the York architect, John Carr, who was the first architect of any significance to practise in Lancashire. He was the son of a mason, quarry owner and building contractor and had been clerk of works for Lord Burlington for a house which the latter had designed near York. He therefore knew more than most architects of his day about the actual construction of buildings, as distinct from the design of their façades and main rooms, and had also learned how to design in the fashionable Classical style of the day which we now call 'Palladian' – after the sixteenth-century Venetian architect, Andrea Palladio, whom many Georgian architects regarded as their master and sole source of all 'correct' architectural design.

As one approaches the house through the woodland which hides it from view until almost the last moment, it appears a typically Palladian building of brick with stone dressings. Its ground-floor windows have

what are called Gibbs surrounds – after the architect who made them popular – in which every other stone is not carved to shape but left square. This was meant to give an idea of heaviness and solidity appropriate in the basement of a building; the front door has Doric details for the same reason. In contrast, the windows of the first and second floors have smoothly finished surrounds, and the giant columns which rise between them in the centre of the façade are of the more graceful Ionic order. The pediment is intended to give due emphasis to the centre of the building, while the slightly projecting quoins give an appearance of greater solidity to the ends.

Everything gives the impression that, according to the contemporary fashion, the state rooms are on the first floor (for which eighteenth-century gentry used the Italian phrase 'il piano nobile') while the ground floor (which was often called 'the rustick') was given over to rooms for the servants and rooms which the family used for their normal daily life, when they were not expecting important guests who had to be impressed. But Lytham Hall is, like Gawthorpe Hall (which I described in the previous chapter) more than usually interesting, because it is a

Lytham Hall

house which stands at the turning point between an older tradition and a newer fashion: all the state rooms except the best bedroom – and even that was probably used by the owner and his wife – were on the ground floor. In part this was possible because Lytham Hall was built in front of an early seventeenth-century house, which was then converted into a service courtyard.

Visitors, unless they are VIPs being entertained by the GRE, now go into the house through the side doorway into a vestibule which originally led on the left to the family sitting room and on the right to the library, both pleasantly panelled rooms with otherwise little decoration. The side doorway was probably the normal way-in for members of the family in the eighteenth century, but on special occasions, or when there were guests to accommodate, the front door was opened to give access to the Hall.

As at Towneley this was designed to be a most imposing entry, aiming to show that the young Thomas Clifton – he was about thirty when the house was begun – had pretensions to be the most important landowner in the Fylde. The room is some twenty-five feet square and about twelve feet high and decorated with a restrained opulence, from the stone-flagged floor with square insets of

'marble' to the ceiling where rectangular panels are decorated with luxurious acanthus scrolls in low relief. On the walls the decoration is concentrated on and above the fireplace, with garlands and drops of flowers, and on the doorcases which are given Doric details to stress the fact that this is the lowest storey of the house.

Through the mahogany door, which stands opposite, one comes at first into an open-sided corridor, which links all the main rooms on the ground floor, and then through a screen of two Ionic columns, into the lower half of the stair hall, a most imposing space, about twenty-five feet square and somewhat higher. The staircase itself has three balusters of turned mahogany on each tread and rises in the centre of the hall in a single flight to a half-landing from which two flights rise in the opposite direction up the side walls – a form which, because of its magnificence, is called 'imperial'. The walls are decorated with plaster panels of which four contain drops modelled in fairly high relief representing archery, hunting, shooting and the arts, regarded as the ideal pursuits of a country gentleman.

But the best is yet to come. Looking up, above the 'Venetian' window with its round-headed central light and lower flat-headed

Lytham Hall – Staircase Ceiling

side lights, one sees that the stair hall rises through a square dome to a flat panel surrounded by rich scrollwork and decorated with a coloured bas-relief of the god Jupiter sitting majestically on the clouds of heaven, accompanied by an eagle and carrying a sceptre and a pair of thunderbolts. Why? Why should a Catholic squire on the edge of the Fylde surround himself with all this architectural splendour and Roman mythology?

I wrote a few pages back that educated men in the seventeenth and eighteenth centuries looked back across the middle age of 'gothic'

Lytham Hall – Dining Room

darkness to the time of the Roman Empire, which they regarded as a golden age. The great historian, Edward Gibbon, wrote that it had been the time at which more people enjoyed peace and plenty than at any subsequent time; whether he was right or wrong matters less, in this context, than that his contemporaries believed that he was right, and that they regarded themselves as carrying on from where the Romans had been forced to stop by barbarian invaders. Of course, Thomas Clifton did not believe in the god Jupiter any more than we do, but Jupiter was a myth, a symbol of great power well used; he was the creator and sustainer of the universe, the upholder of the moral order and the punisher of wicked men. So Clifton was no doubt flattered when John Carr's favourite plasterer, Giuseppe Cortese, suggested such a design for the most splendid room in the house, for had not he, Thomas Clifton, created fine farmland by the draining of Lytham Moss, and was not he the richest and most powerful man in the Fylde, and a magistrate, a dispenser of justice, as well?

After this splendour the other rooms are something of an anti-climax, but this did not matter. The point had been made, and would have been understood by Clifton's contemporaries; furthermore one cannot live in the grand manner all the time. This is not to say that the family did not live well. All of the bedrooms on the first floor have well-made doors and fine plasterwork chimneypieces, and each had a dressing room en suite. The finest bedroom is not in fact at the top of the stairs, as one would expect, but in the south-east corner of the house where it has a special alcove framed with Doric columns for the bed – and a bathroom which is well worth looking at as a fine example of 1930s decoration.

John Carr designed Lytham Hall and thereafter kept a watchful eye on the progress of the work, but only occasionally and from a distance – it would have taken a good day of hard travelling to get from York to Lytham in the 1750s. Meanwhile he was engaged elsewhere producing designs for houses and public buildings and was also the clerk of works for Robert Adam's interior decoration of Harewood House in Yorkshire. When therefore he came in due course to design the Dining Room and Drawing Room at Lytham, in the 1760s, his design bore many of the hallmarks of Adam's work. Carr was not an arrogant man; he understood that what a house needs most is a convenient plan and secondly sound construction, and that façade design and interior decoration are more matters of changing fashion or taste. That is why he designed the front of the house in the traditional manner to look as though the main rooms were on the first floor, and that is why the Dining Room and Drawing Room have much more delicate motifs in their plasterwork than elsewhere in the house. Taste was changing. People were realising that the interiors of Roman houses, which were then being uncovered for almost the first time at the excavations of Pompeii and Herculaneum, had not been so richly modelled architecturally. They were discovering (thanks in part to Adam himself) that the Romans had used decorative motifs unknown to Renaissance architects like Palladio. They were beginning also to appreciate that Greek architecture had been different again — but English buildings based on Greek designs were (with very few exceptions of which none is in Lancashire) still a generation ahead in the future.

Thomas Clifton wanted to be up-to-date, and John Carr had no objection. He put his aim modestly — 'to arrange the necessary conveniences with some degree of art'. He was therefore willing to use at Lytham motifs in much lower relief like bundles of reeds, garlands of oat-husks, delicately fluted fans and the stylised honeysuckle leaves which one sees in the shallow recess in the Dining Room from which the meals were served. The Drawing Room is decorated with painted panels of 'grotesques' — delicate trails of foliage, small medallions and fabulous beasts like griffons. Such pretty decoration has its strange name, not because it is complicated or mis-shapen, but because it was first discovered during excavations in sixteenth-century Rome, in what were then underground rooms or grottos.

Clifton's hopes were realised: his house became a model for the next generation. Ten miles away on the other side of the Wyre, Alexander Butler had a similar but smaller house built at Kirkland Hall near Churchtown. On the other side of the County near Clitheroe — on John Carr's way from York — the Aspinwall family had their house, Standen Hall, rebuilt at least in part during the 1750s. Richard Gillow, the Lancaster architect, gave his Customs House a façade which is a scaled-down version of the front of Lytham Hall, and the fine house, 4

High Street, Lancaster, which the lawyer John Rawlinson had built around 1770 shows the same influence in its columned doorway, its elaborately framed windows and elegant pediment.

The Palladian style of façade was spreading down the social scale from the gentry to what they called 'the middling sort' of people like lawyers, doctors, parsons and the richer merchants. Such people had in fact been building themselves houses with Classical details for at least a generation, and, though there are fine individual examples of Mid Georgian town houses at Ormskirk (43 Burscough Street) and at Blackburn (39-41 King Street), **Lancaster** is the place to see the best collection.

Lancaster — Ring o' Bells

The Ring o' Bells public house, 54 King Street, was built originally as a private house, probably in the 1740s. It cannot be symmetrical, because it is only four windows wide, but it has a richly moulded façade and the most elaborate doorway in the town, with fluted Doric columns and a fine frieze of rams' heads and military trophies under a segmental pediment. A slightly plainer though symmetrical house stands at 78 Church Street and is now the Conservative Club. Bonnie Prince Charlie is supposed to have stayed here twice in 1745, on the way south and on the retreat north. The doorway, which perhaps welcomed the Young Pretender, has fluted Ionic columns carrying a triangular pediment; what is more interesting is the conical snuffer (to the side of the stairs down to the basement) where footmen would extinguish their torches — a relic of the days when there was no streetlighting.

Melling Hall

front, while the service rooms like the kitchen and dairy are at the back overlooking the farmyard. One of my favourites, built of brick, is the not quite symmetrical Broughton Hall near Preston; in stone there is Knuzden Hall near Blackburn, but virtually every parish in the County has a couple, and many are visible from a public road. The best thing to do is to travel with your eyes open.

I wrote a few paragraphs ago that tastes were changing after the middle of the eighteenth century, that people were becoming aware of, and interested in, a wider variety of decorative motifs than had been available to those architects who regarded Palladio as their master. We are unfortunate in Lancashire that we have no first-class examples to show to the public how this 'neo-classical' design was developed after Lytham Hall; for that one has to go to Heaton Hall near Manchester or Tatton Park near Knutsford. The best which the present County can offer are the pretty ceilings in a solicitor's office built in 1775 at 80 Church Street, Lancaster (which can be glimpsed through the windows of the semi-circular porch), the Regency Rooms at **Towneley Hall,** and the Dining Room and Drawing Room at **Browsholme Hall.**

Both these houses, and especially the Ring o' Bells, have a more pronounced vertical emphasis than Rawlinson's house; in this they are typical of houses of the earlier eighteenth century, before the universal adoption of the Palladian fashion, which, because it was based on Italian precedents, made windows less prominent in walls. The best example I know of this change of fashion and reduced emphasis on windows is at **Melling Hall** (now a hotel). This was built in the early eighteenth century as a five-bay house but was altered around 1775 into one with an elegant new doorway on four Ionic columns and only three windows on the ground and first floors. The original five windows on the second floor survive to this day unchanged, and the 'ghosts' of the original windows on the lower floors can still be seen on either side of those which replaced them.

By the late eighteenth century larger farmers were building themselves such houses – one of the first I know is Bradkirk Hall near Kirkham which is dated 1764; another on the other side of the County is Heyroyd at Colne. Some farmhouses, like Goss House at Arkholme, continued to have mullioned windows despite a Classical doorcase, but by 1800 virtually every farmhouse in the County was being built to look like what has become the traditional dolls' house, with two storeys, tall sash windows on either side of the front door and a minimum of decoration of Classical inspiration. They are no different from middle-sized town houses except that they are freestanding; the family rooms are at the

The rooms at Towneley were designed by Jeffrey Wyatt in 1812. The former Dining Room has a deeply coved ceiling enriched with scrollwork while the Drawing Room is, to my taste, more elegant with a ceiling carried on shallow segmental arches. Jeffrey Wyatt also designed an external passage running underneath the porch so that servants could carry food to the Dining Room from the kitchen on the other side of the house without being seen in the hall. The rooms at Browsholme are much more simple but are filled with roughly contemporary furniture and some nice family portraits. Browsholme Hall could hardly be called one of the great stately homes of England; as at Leighton Hall – of which more in Chapter 7 – a major part of its attraction is that it is not a museum but a family home, and that one is normally shown around by a member of the Parker family who clearly enjoys the task.

One final development remains to be mentioned, and that is the terrace of houses linked together to form a single grouped design. The practice started in London before the Civil War, developed widely there during the Restoration, blossomed in Bath from the late 1720s onward, but was virtually unknown in Lancashire until the end of the eighteenth century. An exception is the group of three brick houses built around 1750 on King Street, Whalley, where they look rather out of place. John Dalton's speculative development of the streets around the Square in Lancaster which bears his name was not a great success — only a few houses as well as a Catholic church were built on the Square to the standard pattern laid down. The best place to see Late Georgian urban housing is therefore at Preston, where the town developed as a thriving manufacturing and administrative centre just as Lancaster's port began to decline around 1800. Winckley Square was laid out about then, though original houses are now few in number, but the streets to the south and south-east contain a number of short terraces, of which perhaps the most attractive is Bushell Place. The houses there were built (without bay windows) in about 1825 to front onto a broad esplanade which had been laid out by the Corporation as long ago as 1698. By far the finest single development is **Richmond Terrace** in **Blackburn,** which dates from 1838 and has Ionic doorways with a frieze and cornice set under brick arches.

Another street of attractive small terraced houses with vaguely Classical details is **Bath Street** in **Lytham,** where the old town was developed in the first half of the nineteenth century by the Cliftons of Lytham Hall. What singles these houses in Lytham out as worth a visit is not the houses themselves, but the

Lytham — Bath Street

contemporary decorative **pebble pavements** outside them. Pebbles (rather than flagstones) for pavements and cobbles (rather than setts) for carriageways were common in the early nineteenth century, but these decorative pavements seem to have been a speciality of Lytham, for there are traces in other streets. Each house in Bath Street is graced with a different pattern: a sailing boat and a windmill as reminders of the locality, but also a star, some flowers and some birds.

Some of the most interesting buildings in the Classical tradition are not houses at all: I have already mentioned the Customs House at Lancaster. The reason for this is that the scope of architectural design, as distinct from mere building in the traditional manner, was greatly extended during the eighteenth century — but that is a subject large enough for another chapter.

Blackburn — Richmond Terrace

Chapter Five
The Extension of the
Classical Tradition

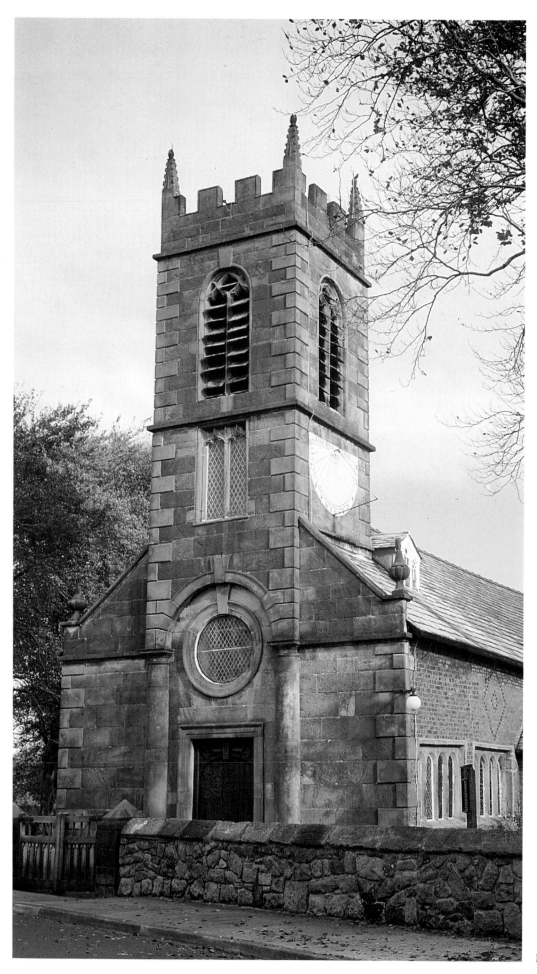

Much Hoole Church

5. THE EXTENSION OF THE CLASSICAL TRADITION

Poulton Church

The **parish church** of **St. Chad** in **Poulton-le-Fylde** is best seen on a morning in early spring when the crocuses are in flower in the churchyard and the gilded weathervane — shaped like a ship to remind us that Poulton was once a port — gleams against a pale blue sky; but it is also worth visiting during any of the other fifty weeks in the year. Its chancel was built in 1868 with a rounded end to look like the chancel of a church built in the twelfth century; its tower was also somewhat backward-looking in its design; it was built in the early seventeenth century, but could have been built at almost any time in the previous 150 years. Between the tower and the chancel is the nave which, when it was completed in 1753, was, if not right up to date, at least not out of fashion.

It is a plain building, but clearly in the Classical tradition — its façade on the side facing the Market Square is so composed as to be virtually symmetrical with two central windows flanked by doorways with oval windows over them and another window just beyond. The two doorways — on the left for the congregation and on the right for the vicar — have portals formed by a pair of Doric columns carrying a pediment. Beyond the vicar's door, however, is another with its pediment carried on nicely scrolled brackets; this bears the date 1699 and the name of Richard Fleetwood, for it leads to the burial vault of the Fleetwoods of Rossall Hall. Richard Fleetwood's heiress, Margaret,

married Roger Hesketh of Meols, near Southport (which did not exist then) and the couple paid for the rebuilding of the nave. The rainwater hoppers bear their coat of arms and the date 1753, and there are several memorial tablets inside to members of their family.

It is inside that the differences between this church and what one might call a typical medieval church are obvious, for the space has a single overall roof and no subdivisions except for the widely spaced Doric columns carrying the gallery which runs around three sides. This has a panelled front and is approached up a fine staircase in the north-west corner. The church, when built, did not have a chancel as it does now, though there may have been a small recess for the communion table. Instead, where the chancel arch now is, there stood the pulpit (as is the case in many Nonconformist churches) for the most important part of the services in the Church of England was then the sermon. Churches became essentially auditoriums with a clear and uninterrupted view of the parson in his pulpit.

Poulton Church was not rebuilt until two hundred years after the Reformation, but very few new churches were built in that time. There were, quite simply, enough medieval churches which could be modified according to the necessities of the new style of Protestant worship in the Church of

England, which stressed the singing of hymns and psalms, prayers and a sermon rather than the sharing of bread and wine around the communion table. Almost all of the few churches which were built follow the same open plan as at Poulton, and their differences are largely ones of scale; they are also similar in that by the beginning of the eighteenth century such decoration as they have is based on the motifs of Classical architecture. The theme of this chapter is how what one might loosely call the 'Classical Style' spread over all aspects of architectural design, in traditional building types like churches and bridges and in new types of building which had to be evolved, as society developed and became more complicated.

The earliest post-Reformation parish church in Lancashire is **St. Leonard's** at **Samlesbury** which was built (or, rather, rebuilt) in 1558; the tower dates from 1900. In its style the church continues the medieval tradition with arches and aisles, but its fittings date largely from the seventeenth century. It has a very full complement of box pews (bearing dates between 1678 and 1756, though some must be earlier) as well as a communion rail of turned balusters. This was probably made as a direct result of Archbishop Laud's orders in 1634 that communion tables should be protected from 'profaneness', that is, the attention of dogs who came with their masters to church; but, like so many others, it has been kept as an aid to kneeling and rising.

The next earliest church is at Much Hoole, but, before looking at this, it is worthwhile to travel mentally to the other side of the County, to **Slaidburn**, a most attractive village of stone-built cottages and cobbled pavements in the heart of the Forest of Bowland. Here **St. Andrew's** is another late-medieval parish church of no great beauty redeemed by the considerable interest of its fittings, which have remained virtually unchanged for well over two hundred years. Most of the nave is filled with seventeenth-century pews; some are dated, and others bear the initials of the families who used them. There are also eighteenth-century box pews — less draughty for the richer families who rented them — and a fine three-decker pulpit, installed in 1740. Most such pulpits were reduced in height in Victorian times when box pews were removed to restore a more medieval appearance to churches, so this one is something of a rarity; I know of only one other in the County. The parson

conducted the service from the middle tier, or lectern, while the parish clerk led the congregation's responses from the bottom stall, and, when the time came for the parson to preach, he climbed the nicely balustraded stair to the pulpit, which stands on four columns and has a sounding board to help his voice to be heard more clearly.

To the east of the pulpit is perhaps the most interesting feature of the church. This is the Jacobean chancel screen, which is unique in the County. It was placed there, probably in the 1630s, in response to Archbishop Laud's orders that the Church of England should revert to something approaching the style of worship of pre-Reformation days, with a screen (like the old rood screen) to separate the priest in his chancel from the people in their nave. This screen is a fine piece with tapering square uprights closely carved with geometric patterns and carrying semi-circular arches which support an openwork balustrade. Laud's reactionary reforms hardly outlived his execution in 1645 (for alleged treason) but the screen remained — I imagine, because it gave an extra distinction to the family pews next to it.

Slaidburn Church – Pulpit

St. Michael's Church at **Much Hoole** is dated 1628 on the doorway inside its porch. This also contains two boards painted with the Lord's Prayer and the Ten Commandments, which must originally have been placed on the wall on either side of the

Much Hoole Church

Pilling – Old St. John's Church

communion table at the east end, as was normally the case. For nearly a century the church was a simple brick building on a stone plinth, looking hardly different from a single storey house with mullioned windows; inside, it is simple too, with box pews, an early nineteenth-century gallery, a tall-backed pulpit with a sounding board dated 1695, and a plain octagonal font donated in 1663 by John Stones who lived at Carr House, Bretherton. All this simplicity was made more sophisticated in 1722 when the slender tower was built to the west of the church, with its east wall resting within the church on an arch carried by two sturdy Tuscan columns (which are simpler than Doric ones). These are repeated as the main motif on the west front and are flanked by flaming urns, which were also added to the porch.

On the south of the tower is a painted sundial, dated 1875 but probably older, while on the other side is a clock which serves as a memorial to Jeremiah Horrocks. He was the curate here in 1639, when on 24 November he became the first man to witness and describe what astronomers now know as the Transit of Venus — the passing of the planet Venus in front of the face of the Sun. This was not a mere incident in the history of astronomy, but a significant event in Man's evolving appreciation of his place in the Universe, for it helped to prove Copernicus' theory that, whatever our eyes appear to see, the planets including the Earth do rotate around the Sun, and that the traditional view, which made the Earth, and therefore Man, the centre of the Universe, was wrong.

Before the tower was built at Much Hoole, the church presumably looked much like **Old St. John's Church** at **Pilling** with its bellcote at the west end. This church, which stands in what is still the parish graveyard with a good complement of yew trees, is no longer used for regular worship, since it was replaced in 1887 by the fine church of St. John about two hundred yards to the north – of which more in Chapter 7. It is now in the care of that remarkable organisation, the Redundant Churches Fund, which is financed by the Church of England and the Department of the Environment to look after churches which are no longer required, but are too precious for one reason or another to be demolished or converted. Pilling Old Church is precious, not because of its architectural quality, for that is fairly minimal, but because it is a virtually unchanged example of a church which was designed for the worship of God according to the Church of England's Book of Common Prayer and was not spoilt in Victorian times by 'restoration' to what people then thought was a more worthy and appropriate place of worship. It is not always open, but the windows have plain glass, so that the interior is fairly easy to see.

The church was built of soft red sandstone (which outcrops only rarely in the Fylde) with dressings of the more common and harder gritstone. These include the approximately Ionic 'capitals' on the doorway which is dated 1717. Inside, everything is of that date except the north and west galleries, which probably date from the early nineteenth century and are supported on timber Tuscan columns. The floor is flagged, the walls are limewashed, the pews are unvarnished oak and provide no more than a seat, a back and a pair of ends; there are a couple of box pews for the 'better' families; the pulpit is a three-decker with simple panels and there is a railing of turned balusters to protect the communion table. It

is almost a time capsule for a simpler, less pretentious though probably more bigoted age; I find it easy to picture in my mind's eye the village parson in his wig and Geneva bands climbing to the lectern to begin Mattins in Cranmer's immortal prose and climbing further to the pulpit to deliver a sermon of well-rounded sentences.

A more sophisticated version of this sort of church is **St. Mary's** which stands by the A59 at **Tarleton,** where it was built in 1719. It too has been taken into the care of the Redundant Churches Fund, having been used as the cemetery chapel after the building of a new church in the village about a hundred years ago. It is built of brick (which was originally rendered) because there is no stone in the lowlands of West Lancashire. Its side walls are completely symmetrical with four round-headed windows separated by triangular pilasters. The entrance is at the west end through a more recent porch; originally the porch seems to have been in the base of the bell-tower, which was raised in stone in 1824 and presumably crowned then with the pretty little rotunda carried on Doric columns. At the east end is a semi-octagonal bay which contains the communion table; outside, it has a rainwater hopper carrying the arms of the Banastre family from Bank Hall, who presumably paid for the cost of the building. The interior of the church can be visited, by application to the keyholder who lives nearby. It has a panelled west gallery, which is supported on two square fluted pillars and is extended in a matching style halfway along the south wall.

Tarleton Church

Neither Pilling nor Tarleton church approaches Poulton church in the quality of its design, but a church which does is **St. Anne's** at **Woodplumpton.** The interior of the church is of a fairly standard late-medieval type, pleasing but of no great interest except that it has three parallel roofs; but the south aisle was refronted and a small west tower was built in 1748. The tower is lower than the one at Tarleton and is more sturdy, in that it is square and has a cupola carried, not on slender columns, but on solid little piers and arches. Its window has a Gibbs surround. The designer's interest in the sculptural quality of his architectural details – which was rather old-fashioned in 1748 – is also shown in his treatment of the south wall. This has massive Tuscan pilasters at either end, a strongly moulded cornice and two doorways where the protective cornice is carried on a prominent keystone and a complicated assortment of heavily scrolled brackets.

Newchurch-in-Pendle

Woodplumpton Church

A church where the Georgian interior is of more interest than the outside is **St. Mary's** at **Newchurch-in-Pendle** which was rebuilt in 1740. The masons of 1740 are named on a plaque between the third and fourth windows on the south side. The church was probably **new** in the early sixteenth century when it was built as a chapel of ease, that is, a more convenient place of worship in an outlying part of a parish – in this case the large parish based on St Michael's chapel in Clitheroe Castle. The church is interesting outside, for the plain unbuttressed west tower is dated both 1653 and 1712 and has an oval opening on the west face which is locally nicknamed the Eye of God; the east end has a

Venetian window which is also an important feature inside behind the altar. The interior is very pleasing, and unusual in that it is divided down the middle into the nave and a north aisle, but the six-bay arcade of Doric columns which divides them is also unusual because of the quality of its stonework – which is not dressed smooth but slightly fluted on each face, so that there is a delicate play of light and shade across the surface of the columns and arches; it is a beautiful piece of work. The gallery behind it on the north and the one to the west are also pleasing in the quality of their panelled fronts, and there is a fine brass chandelier.

I suspect that St. Mary's was rebuilt 1740 because the original church was too small; similarly, the **parish church** at **Edenfield,** which has a tower rather like the one at Newchurch and apparently dated 1614, must have been rebuilt in 1778 to accommodate a growing population of textile workers in the Irwell Valley. As such it is typical of several churches in the area; the churches of St. James at Church and at Accrington are other examples. It was obviously designed to have galleries from the start, since the windows on both the north and south sides are in two tiers. Inside, it has the wide open space I remarked on at Poulton-le-Fylde, two fine chandeliers, and panelled galleries on three sides which are carried on slim cast-iron columns above sets of box pews in the north and south aisles. The chancel is slightly deeper than any other we have seen before and has a Venetian window, but of the pulpit for which this auditorium was built there is no sign: my guess is that it was placed in the centre of the church just to the west of the chancel arch, and that the box pews which presumably filled the central space were set back around it.

Lancaster — St. John's Church

This was certainly the case in what is my favourite Georgian church, **St. John's** at **Lancaster,** which is also now in the care of the Redundant Churches Fund. It was opened in 1755 on a site on the Green Ayre given by the Corporation (who also paid for the box pews and galleries) in order to serve the growing population of the eastern parts of the town — and no doubt too in the hope of arresting the spread of religious Nonconformity, or Dissent as it was known in the eighteenth-century. The architect is not known, but he produced a simple though accomplished design with façades which were originally symmetrical, a semi-circular apse at the east end for the communion table, and an interior in which the chancel and nave, the ground floor and the galleries are neatly linked together: the inner edges of the galleries are supported on square pillars, above which rise slender Ionic columns to carry the cornice which runs around the whole of the major space and carries the coved ceiling.

This basic arrangement was virtually unchanged in 1875, when a wrought-iron pulpit was substituted for the original one (whose sounding board I found in the tower a few years ago) and the box pews were slightly cut down and given raking rather than upright backs. The communion rail remains, and what I believe was the original communion table is in the north chapel. On the gallery at the west end stands the attractive organ case of 1785. The tower and spire were not part of the original church, but were added in 1784 to the designs of Thomas Harrison, an architect who came from Yorkshire to Lancaster after winning the

competition for Skerton Bridge — of which more later — but eventually moved on to Chester. The Doric rotunda on the top of the tower is his reinterpretation of the motifs of the so-called Choragic Monument of Lysicrates at Athens, built in 334 BC. Harrison, like most younger architects of his day, was interested in the remains of ancient Greek architecture, which were then being revealed for the first time to West European eyes as scholars were allowed to enter the Ottoman Empire. He provided another version of the monument to crown Lancaster's Old Town Hall, which is now the City Museum.

The Church of England has always regarded itself as a reformed Catholic Church and has tried to be the Church of all the English people, steering a middle course which offers the best features of the more traditionally minded priest-led Roman Catholic Church and the Bible-inspired individualism of the Churches of the Protestant denominations. Inevitably, therefore, it has gone too far for some people and not far enough for others, and its attempts to establish a consensus of belief and uniformity of practice — often, it must be admitted, by force — have met with resistance, sometimes passive and at other times more active and even violent. To simplify somewhat excessively, in the sixteenth century most resistance came from Roman Catholics who disliked the changes made; in the seventeenth, especially after the Restoration, it came more from Protestants who feared that these changes might be unmade. By the eighteenth century a compromise was tacitly accepted whereby people who did not wish to worship in Anglican churches could opt out, provided that they did so fairly discreetly and were ready to accept that the price they had to pay was virtual exclusion from political life.

In the eighteenth century, then, one finds Nonconformist chapels being built in increasingly large numbers, but, in order not to draw attention to themselves, they were always simple buildings with no architectural pretensions. For that reason, therefore, unless one has a particular religious motive to undertake what amounts to a pilgrimage to a certain place of worship, few early Nonconformist chapels are, in my view, worth making more than a very short détour to see. The best exceptions are at Rivington, Rawtenstall and Yeoland Conyers.

Goodshaw Old Baptist Chapel

Rivington today is a very small village prettily set on sloping ground at the north end of Lever Park above the long line of reservoirs built in the middle of the nineteenth century to supply the people of Liverpool with pure water. In the days before the best land in the parish was flooded, it must have been a place of some importance with a parish church, a grammar school (now at Horwich) and also a **Unitarian Chapel** which was built in 1703. I suppose that most people looking at the chapel today would think that it is a Victorian village school, with its bellcote and symmetrical façade with two big cross-windows flanked by doors, and the two-storey cottage behind. What gives the game away after the first glance is the presence of a graveyard. The chapel is not open during the week, but one can get a glimpse through the windows at the back, which are on either side of the pulpit. What one sees is a plain room simply furnished with box pews, and the pew of the Willoughby family with its high panelled back and Classical cornice immediately opposite, and only just lower than, the pulpit.

Rivington Unitarian Chapel

A similarly arranged church which is normally open to the public, because it is now cared for by English Heritage, is the **Old Baptist Chapel at Goodshaw near Rawtenstall.** This was built in 1760 and then extended forwards in the early nineteenth century — the gable walls show the outline of the original building, while there are smaller, older windows in the back wall. It is clear from the symmetrical front that there are galleries on three sides, and, even if the chapel is shut, one can see them through the lower windows. As at the Unitarian Chapel at Rivington there are two doors, but I do not think that in either chapel men were segregated from women during worship. Between the doors on the inside is the pulpit, with the singers' pew in front of it: music played a large part in the worship at Goodshaw.

In all the churches and chapels, which we have looked at so far, the pulpit is the most important feature, because both Anglicans and Dissenters shared the view that the most important part of the Sunday service was the regular exposition of the Word of God to the congregation by a trained minister or priest. The exception to this practice is provided by the Society of Friends (or Quakers) who, as the title of the Society suggests, regarded (and still regard) themselves as a community who needed no priests, because all were equally open to the promptings of the Spirit of God: it was sufficient to meet together on the morning of each First Day and wait in thoughtful silence until a member felt moved by God to lead his (or her) friends in worship by speaking or praying.

Friends' Meeting Houses, at least in Lancashire, go back further than any other Nonconformist places of worship. The Meeting House in Lancaster has a datestone of 1677, though nothing substantial remains from that time. My favourite **Friends' Meeting House** is at **Yealand Conyers** and is set in a well-tended graveyard which has regular rows of simple headstones and the feel of a cottage garden. It was built in 1692 but damaged by fire in the mid-eighteenth century and partly rebuilt; only the datestone on the porch and an upper window to the right reveal its pre-Georgian origins. The two doors are nicely panelled — though badly disfigured with well-carved initials, including one dated 1775 — and lead to the meeting room itself which has twelve-pane sash windows and well-made panelling with fluted pilasters.

We are used to regard Nonconformity as meaning beliefs and practices which are more Protestant than those of the Anglican Church but, strictly speaking, the term should include Roman Catholicism as well. I doubt that such an open-minded view would have been acceptable before the late eighteenth century, because Roman Catholicism was long (and, mostly, unjustly) associated with treason — with the wish to assassinate the excommunicated Queen Elizabeth, to blow up the Houses of Parliament in 1605, and to support the Stuarts in 1715 and 1745. It was not until 1778 that the building of Roman Catholic churches in towns and villages (as distinct from country houses) was officially tolerated, and it took some time for small congregations and their gentry supporters to find the money, and the courage, to take advantage of the law. The earliest Catholic church still in use in Lancashire is (I think) St. Peter and St. Paul's Church at Stydd near Ribchester, which dates from 1798. It has more historical than architectural interest, although the way in which the church balances an outbuilding to the presbytery, so that each appears to be one of a pair of pavilions to the house, is neatly handled.

Most Catholic churches are open during the daylight hours, but many of the early ones have been substantially altered by the same Victorian love of decorative rather than architectural richness which spoilt many Anglican churches in the latter half of the nineteenth century. Perhaps the church which still gives the most faithful impression of those built in the classical tradition is **St. Mary's** at **Chipping.** It was built in 1827 and,

Yealand Conyers Friends' Meeting House

typically, is attached to its presbytery which stands behind it. Outside, it is a simple building with five tall round-headed windows. Inside, it is a single open space, without the galleries which one associates with Protestant churches — presumably because congregations were smaller — and is designed in such a way that the priest at the altar in the shallow chancel is clearly visible, if not audible, to everyone in the congregation. The importance of the chancel, where the miracle of the Mass was believed to take place, is emphasised by four Corinthian columns which link the chancel arch and the lower arches on either side in such a way as to suggest a triumphal arch, while the altar itself is flanked by four more Corinthian columns — an order always associated with splendour and rejoicing.

Chipping Catholic Church

Chorley – St. Gregory's Catholic Church

Another Catholic church which exults in this way is **St. Gregory's** at **Chorley** where the chancel is merely a shallow extension to the nave, which is surrounded by Corinthian pilasters. The most interesting feature of the church, which was built in 1815 and extended with aisles in 1831, is the entrance and the tower above it which were built in good quality stonework in 1845. This façade does not really match the interior, for it gives the impression that it stands directly in front of low aisles and a taller nave. Nevertheless, it looks rather fine and somewhat Italian, as the tower rises above the 'nave' with two pilasters bearing a pediment around each bell opening under the lead-covered dome.

Several of these Catholic churches have schools built very close to them, as indeed is often the case with Anglican churches, because the links between the churches and education have always been close. Lancaster Royal Grammar School traces its continuous existence back to the priest of a chantry founded in 1469 by John Gardiner of Bailrigg, which is now the site of Lancaster University; he was required not merely to sing masses for the souls of Gardiner and his relatives but also to instruct local boys in the rudiments of Latin. Until 1851 the school building stood a few yards to the west of St. Mary's Church. If old drawings can be believed, it resembled the seventeenth-century grammar school which survives at

Earby and now houses an interesting small **museum of mining.** This looks like a middle-sized farmhouse of the period with a two-storey gabled porch. What suggests that it is not a farmhouse is the fact that the chimney stacks are at either end, which probably means that the schoolmaster had a two-storey house to the right, while the school room was on the ground floor to the left and rather like a big hall. This is not so strange as it may seem, because a new building type has always been accommodated at first in a traditionally designed building, minimally modified to suit the new use; only later have the shortcomings (if any) of such an approach led to further experiments to find a more ideal design solution.

A more sophisticated building is the former Grammar School (now a **primary school**) by the church at **Slaidburn** which, according to the inscription, 'Was Erected and Endowed by JOHN BRENNAND, late of Panehill in this Parish, Gentleman, who died the 15th day of May in the Year of Our LORD 1717'. This inscription is situated above the doorway, which has a segmental pediment carried on fluted pilasters and forms the centre of a nine-bay façade; all the windows have the cross of mullion and transom which was fashionable in gentry houses until the end of the seventeenth century. A school which looks even more like a contemporary house is the early building of

Clitheroe Grammar School, which dates from 1782 but was moved to its present site stone by stone in wheelbarrows in 1834. It stood originally near St. Mary's parish church and looks no different from several of the other Late Georgian houses on Church Street.

In the early nineteenth century concern for the better provision of primary education for the children of a growing population exercised the minds of many people, not least James Kay whom I have mentioned in connection with Gawthorpe Hall. He was particularly active in the 1830s and 1840s and was able to build on the work of two major societies already in the field, the National Society for Anglicans and the British and Foreign School Society for Nonconformists. Many of the present Church of England primary schools in the County originated as National Schools, but I cannot think of any one which it is worth going out of one's way to see – quite apart from which most were built with Gothic rather than Classical details. So my favourite **primary school** of the period is at **Broughton** and was built by the Roman Catholics, a stone's throw away from their church at Fernyhalgh. In the same way that the presbytery and church at Stydd were neatly linked together into a single design of a centre block with pavilions, so too this school has a central two-storey house (presumably for the master) flanked by a pair of single-storey wings. These project at right angles and have pilasters at the corners and Classical pediments instead of normal gables. Since they are labelled GIRLS and BOYS

respectively, they must have been the main classrooms. It is a very attractive little composition which bears the date MDCCCXXXVI on the parapet of the house: 1836 almost marks the end of the Classical tradition in Lancashire.

In the days before the Welfare State, people with Christian consciences as well as money were often reminded by their priest or minister of the Parable of the Good Samaritan and thereby encouraged to look after the poor, the elderly or those who had fallen on hard times. The earliest almshouses in Lancashire are the Croston Almshouses on Town Lane, Croston and bear the date 1692, though I find it difficult to believe that much of the present fabric dates from so long ago. Much more impressive are the **Shireburne Almshouses** at **Hurst Green** which were founded in 1706 by Sir Nicholas Shireburne in compliance with the will of his father Richard, who had died in 1689 in prison in Manchester because, as a prominent Roman Catholic, he was suspected of treasonable loyalty to James II. The ten cottages were originally built at Kemple End, a mile or so to the north of Hurst Green at the end of Longridge Fell, but they were dismantled and brought down to a more central location in 1946 and then extended by the addition of an upper storey in the wings. The new work can be clearly seen, since it has low three-light mullioned windows rather than the tall cross-windows of the original building. The centrepiece is decked out with Classical trimmings, with the Shireburne arms under a pediment decorated with three heavily moulded urns. Up its steps and behind its

Broughton – Fernyhalgh School

Hurst Green — Shireburne Almshouses

Stydd — Almshouses

balustrade, it is really rather fine — as much a monument to the taste of the Shireburnes as to their charitable work.

Far less sophisticated are the six **almshouses** at **Stydd,** standing in their garden with a well in front. They were founded under the will of John Shireburne (presumably a minor cousin of the family at Stonyhurst) who died in 1726, and were built of brick with stone dressings around the tall sash windows. Unusually, they had two storeys from the start, and if someone lived on the upper storey — more difficult of access but also less damp — he or she could sit out in the morning sun under a charming balustraded loggia formed by an arcade carried on four Tuscan columns and supporting a gable with curly sides and a flat top. This is really more striking than attractive, but gives the building a character shared by no other in the County.

More old fashioned in their appearance, though very little older, are the cottages which form **Penny's Hospital** in **Lancaster,**

built in 1720 through the generosity of Alderman William Penny for twelve poor old men. The newly recut Latin inscription orders people who have no business there to stay outside, but one can see all one needs through the wrought-iron gates. The gables of the gateway and of the chapel at the other end of the courtyard are even more sinuous in their outline than at Stydd, and the cottages themselves have cross-windows. Nearly twenty years ago the inhabitants moved out to a new building, but in 1974 the old cottages were modernised without altering their appearance at the front and are now occupied once more, though mostly by women. The scheme won an Architectural Heritage Year Award for its architect, Edward Mason.

Charitable bodies are not always renowned for their financial acumen, but in 1759 the Trustees of Penny's Hospital built the Assembly Rooms next door (to the right) to provide the charity with an additional income from dances and other social events, especially when the County Town was full of gentry at the time of the thrice-yearly Assizes. The lower half of the building, accessible through the semi-circular porch, now houses a variety of market stalls, but the upper room is not yet open to the public. More's the pity, because it is an attractive and well-lit room, half-panelled and with a strong cornice and coved ceiling. At one end is a

musicians' gallery with a panelled front decorated with the geometrical fretwork motifs now called Chinese Chippendale.

Perhaps the finest of all the almshouses of any date in the County are **Bushell's Hospital,** next to the parish church at **Goosnargh;** the reason is that they were built as a house in 1722 – the date is on the rainwater hoppers – and not as almshouses. The change occurred because William Bushell (who came from a wealthy Preston family and was the Rector of Heysham as well as the Curate of Goosnargh) stipulated in his will – he died in 1735 – that if his heiress Elizabeth, who was then eight years old, died before the age of twenty-one without any children of her own, the whole of his estate should be devoted to the foundation of an almshouse at Goosnargh, at or near his father's house, for the maintenance of 'gentlemen or gentlewomen or persons of the better rank of the towns or townships of Preston, Euxton, Goosnargh, Whittingham, Fulwood and Elston'. Fortunately for the gentlefolk of the area, Elizabeth died in 1745, and the house was converted and now could well be regarded as her memorial. It was enlarged three times in the nineteenth century, but an engraving published in 1871 shows that the original house was fairly substantial all the same. Neither the bay windows on either side of the door, nor the wing on the right, nor the double pediments over the centre were there; instead the centre and left-hand wing were crowned with a line of urns like those on the gatepiers. If we make these changes in our mind's eye, we can see before us the fine and fashionable Early Georgian house of a wealthy provincial gentleman.

Lancaster – Penny's Almshouses

Goosnargh – Bushell's Hospital

There was nothing strange in the eighteenth century in converting a building to another use, and there was nothing unusual in giving a new building type the traditional form of a house. The accommodation required by most activities could be provided within the shell of a house, larger or smaller as the circumstances required; and this is what normally happened. The former Dispensary on Castle Hill in Lancaster is a good example. It was built in 1785 to provide free medicines and other medical help for poor people, but looks just like a house of that date. The only things which set it apart originally are the now virtually illegible painted inscription above the datestone in the centre of the first floor and the Coade stone bas-relief representing the Good Samaritan, which was there before the datestone, to remind the better-off of their Christian obligations to their less fortunate neighbours in the community. This plaque was moved, when the Dispensary was moved in 1832, and can now be seen over the main entrance to the Royal Lancaster Infirmary.

My second example is what was built in 1816 as the County Lunatic Asylum and is now the Old Wing of the Moor Hospital in Lancaster. For obvious reasons, it is not open to the public, but the building can be glimpsed across its parkland setting on the south side of Quernmore Road and could easily be mistaken for a country house whose Doric columns and pediment give it a somewhat dour appearance. It was built in Lancaster because the Corporation, at a time when the town had recently lost its position as the administrative centre of the County

and was afraid that it might lose the Assizes too, offered the site to the County authorities, rather than see the Asylum built near Liverpool. The offer was accepted, and Lancaster began a new career as a centre for the care of the mentally handicapped as well as of the physically ill. A similar offer of land was made in the 1960s – though not by the City Council – with the result that Lancashire's University is at Lancaster and' not at Blackpool.

We are unfortunate in Lancashire that we have very few public buildings dating from Georgian times when, to my mind, architectural design reached a peak of beauty, structural soundness and convenience of plan only seldom approached in subsequent generations. I have mentioned the Assembly Rooms in Lancaster and, in the next chapter, shall describe the Customs House on St. George's Quay, but there are only five more worth mentioning.

The so-called Old Town Hall at Ormskirk stands out from its nondescript neighbours in Church Street by virtue of having a rainwater hopper with the date 1779 and the initials ED, and a pediment decorated with the Stanley coat of arms. I assume, therefore, that it was built by the Earl of Derby. A more impressive building is the **former Town Hall at Garstang.** This was built in the late 1750s just along the road from the old Market Cross, a Tuscan column with a ball on top – like the ones at Poulton-le-Fylde and Churchtown. Like most town halls before the Municipal Reform Act of 1835 the one at Garstang was basically a covered market with a meeting room above, but the façade has that mixture of elegance and robustness which I associate with the mid-eighteenth century. The ground floor was originally formed of an open arcade, and the openings on the main façade are composed in the manner of a triumphal arch with rusticated stonework; the meeting room on what in a country house would have been called the 'piano nobile' has tall windows with smoothly moulded architraves and a pediment over the central one – small details which would not have gone unnoticed a couple of centuries ago.

It is not mere Lancaster chauvinism which makes me assert that the finest eighteenth-century public building in the present County is the **Old Town Hall** in **Lancaster,** which now houses the **City Museum.** I

Garstang – Cross and former Town Hall

readily admit that it is not in the same league as Liverpool Town Hall, which was designed by John Wood in 1749 and later extended by James Wyatt, but Liverpool has not been part of Lancashire since 1880. Like its counterpart in Garstang, the Town Hall at Lancaster was originally open on the ground floor behind an arcade and served as a covered market to the west of the Market Square. The portico with its giant Doric columns will also have afforded protection to stall holders and gives an air of dignity to the whole building. It was designed in 1781 by Major Thomas Jarratt, of whom virtually nothing is now known; the Corporation were pleased enough with his work to make him a Freeman of the Borough and to offer him a silver casket, but they decided, on the advice of Thomas Harrison, not to build the clock tower which he had designed, and substituted the present cupola (by Harrison). The year 1987 saw major changes to Lancaster's museums, with the reopening of the Ashton Memorial and the extension of the Maritime Museum, but the City Museum is still worth a visit.

Its displays concentrate on the social and economic history of the town and surrounding area, culminating in a fine collection of old photographs and three models of the town based on the old maps dated 1610, 1778 and 1821. They also include some spectacular Roman finds and the seventh-century shroud and boat-shaped

coffin found in 1973 when the car park near the Jubilee Tower (on the Trough of Bowland road) was being laid out. There is also a special section on the history of the Royal King's Own (Lancaster) Regiment.

The latest of the County's major Georgian public buildings is the **Corn Exchange** in **Preston,** a building which has been surrounded by controversy longer than I can remember, since it lies athwart the line of the extension of the inner ringroad and lost its raison d'être when the new Guild Hall was opened in 1972. The County Planning Department has been able to secure a compromise whereby the rear two-thirds of the building — which contain the rather fine late Victorian Public Hall, designed for concerts and dances — will be demolished, while the original building of 1822 will survive and be refurbished. Not everyone will agree, but I believe this to be the more important part of the whole building, since it is now almost the oldest building in the town, and is also of considerable importance to the townscape: it half-closes the view down Lune Street and will thus reduce the visual impact of the Ringway which, with its surrounding new buildings, is never likely to be regarded as part of the County's architectural heritage.

Lancaster – Old Town Hall

Preston – Corn Exchange

Like most of Preston's major buildings which were constructed before the large-scale exploitation of the stone quarries at Longridge, the Corn Exchange is built of brick with stone dressings — probably to the designs of the contractor William Corry. As one would expect of a building at the end of the Georgian era, its architectural embellishment is reduced to a minimum — a projecting centre with a pediment, chamfered quoins at all the angles, and a Tuscan doorway to suggest that this was a workaday building, which it was. The superb cast-iron gates on either side used to open to give access to the market, while the central doorway led through to an open courtyard which was lined on two storeys by galleries with shops where farmers from the Fylde, the granary of Lancashire, could offer their corn to the merchants and strike what they hoped would be a profitable bargain.

I must briefly mention one other Late Georgian public building in **Preston,** not because it is particularly attractive but because it contains one of the most interesting of the County's museums. It began life as the Sessions House, or court-house, in 1829, but was converted recently and opened in 1987 as the **County and Regimental Museum** in **Stanley Street.** The story of three Lancashire regiments during three centuries is evoked with the aid of uniforms, weapons, medals and a Victorian officers' mess; but what I find more interesting are the displays on Lancashire's

Lytham Mill

history from medieval times which form, as it were, the background to this book. There are sections on castles, monasteries, gentry families and country houses, and also on the development of the services now provided by the County Council — education, the police, roads, the fire brigade and social services. Several of the displays are not so much for looking at as for walking through or experiencing more directly — perhaps the most striking is the Victorian police cell from Darwen!

We have grown so used in recent years to buying our bread in shops and supermarkets, supplied from large-scale centralised bakeries, that we tend to forget how localised were the daily lives of people less than a couple of centuries ago. Every farmhouse and many a cottage had its own bread oven, and the flour for the bread was locally ground from locally grown corn — wheat in the west, and oats in the cooler, wetter Pennine foothills. To the best of my knowledge there is now only one water-powered cornmill in the County, but it is not in working order and not open to the public; so the mill at Chipping which has been converted into a restaurant named after its waterwheel is the next best thing, but it hardly compares with Heron Mill at Beetham in Cumbria which actually works to produce its own flour. In the west of the County, however, there are at least fifteen windmill towers still standing. Several have been converted into houses, though some are empty shells; the most photographed is probably the mill by the canal at Parbold; but the only two worth travelling any distance to see are — appropriately — in the Fylde.

Both were probably built by the same millwright, Ralph Slater of Pilling. **Marsh Mill** at **Thornton** is dated 1794 on the lintel of its door which also names the owner, Bold Fleetwood-Hesketh. **Lytham Mill** on the **East Beach** was built about ten years later. It stands complete with its sails and the ingenious arrangement at the back whereby, if the wind moved one way or the other, it made the fantail spin backwards or forwards and thus drive a system of gearwheels at the base of the boat-shaped cap which turned the sails to face the wind again. As I write these words in the summer of 1988, Marsh Mill has no sails, but by 1989 they should have been replaced, with the result that the mill, which (unlike Lytham's) has all its machinery, will be open to the public in full working order.

83

stands on Tuscan columns which are said to be Roman, but to my mind the most appealing feature is the figure of the white bull himself who stands on a bracket above the front door and looks as though he has just stepped out of a Noah's ark.

Most other old pubs look like houses, but this is not surprising; the Hesketh Arms at Rufford, which must date from the 1790s when the New Hall was built, is perhaps the most pleasing example. It has an extension of two tall storeys to the left which was probably built to provide dining-rooms for travellers on the recently-opened turnpike from Preston to Liverpool, with perhaps a ballroom above. The most attractive Late Georgian public houses I know are the Warners' Arms in Accrington, which has two shallow bow windows flanking the main door, and the Ridgway Arms at Adlington, which has similar bows and a doorway whose head is an ogee-shaped arch.

I have spent much of this chapter writing about new types of buildings and want to finish with a quick look at a traditional building type whose designs were more and more influenced by the Classical tradition as the eighteenth century grew longer – bridges.

The oldest bridges in the County – at Edisford, Paythorne and Whalley, for example – must be medieval in origin though much rebuilt, and no-one knows exactly how old they are. The quaintest

Ribchester – White Bull

From public buildings to public houses is but a slip of the tongue or pen. The oldest ones in the County I have already mentioned as former houses – Heysham Old Hall, the White Bear at Barrowford and the Ring o' Bells in Lancaster. What may well be the oldest pub which was built as an inn is the White Bull at Ribchester. This has a lintel dated 1707, but it is not in its original position, and the building itself has suffered a number of changes. Its two-storey porch

Wycoller – Packhorse Bridge

Lower Hodder Bridge

bridge in the County, which is probably among the oldest as well, is the **packhorse bridge** at **Wycoller.** It is interesting too, in that the stones of which the arches are built run through from side to side. It always looks as though it is on the point of collapse, but it is probably safe enough. There is an old saying that an arch never sleeps, which is a picturesque way of stating that an arch exerts a continuous push outwards; if this is not continuously restrained by a sufficient mass of masonry or other material, the arch will deform. I believe that this is what happened at Wycoller to give the bridge its lopsided look, which so many people have photographed.

This packhorse bridge at Wycoller is so called because, with a width of no more than a yard, it is too narrow to allow the passage of wheeled vehicles. But wheeled vehicles were fairly rare before the end of the eighteenth century; most people travelled on foot or on horseback, and most heavy goods went by water whenever possible and, elsewhere, on the back of a packhorse. (The father of Robert Bindloss, who rebuilt Borwick Hall, made his fortune this way by transporting the fleeces of Westmorland sheep from Kendal to the North Sea ports). The finest packhorse bridge in Lancashire is at **Higherford** with its single high-rising arch spanning the Pendle Water and springing from rocky banks so that

there is little risk of collapse. It was probably built in the 1580s. The most photogenic of these bridges is the old three-arched **Lower Hodder Bridge** between Hurst Green and Great Mitton, which is said to have been built in the 1560s at the expense of Sir Richard Shireburne. John McAdam built a new bridge in 1826, and at some time since then the old bridge lost its parapets, which makes it too dangerous to use but, in its skeletal delicacy, very attractive to look at.

The eighteenth century was the great age of bridge building, but the late seventeenth century made one of the most attractive contributions to the County's architectural heritage in the shape of the **Loyne Bridge** between **Gressingham** and **Hornby.** When it was built in 1684, at the cost of £1250 to the County authorities, it was the only bridge to cross the Lune between Lancaster and Kirkby Lonsdale; any other crossings were made at one of several fords or by the ferry at Arkholme. Loyne Bridge looks little different from most medieval bridges with its three segmental arches rising towards the centre and spanning between triangular cutwaters, which provide a refuge for pedestrians. The same is true of most eighteenth-century bridges, except that in engineering terms they are bolder with the use of arches of a wider span — as can be seen, for example, at Slaidburn or Ribchester.

Penwortham Old Bridge

The prettiest of these eighteenth-century bridges in the County is **Penwortham Old Bridge** which was first built in 1755 by public subscription, to provide a lower crossing of the Ribble than the bridge on the London Road at Walton-le-Dale and thus to facilitate the journey between Preston and the growing port of Liverpool. It collapsed in the following year and was rebuilt in 1759 with a County grant of £2000. Its prettiness arises from the fact that the structure of the bridge and the parapets of the roadway are built of a biscuit-coloured gritstone, whereas the triangular spandrels on either side of the arches are of pink sandstone. Without this it would be no more attractive than any other bridge of its date, though its historical interest would remain intact.

The earliest bridge in Lancashire which one could call beautiful is **Skerton Bridge** in **Lancaster.** It was designed, as I remarked earlier, by Thomas Harrison in 1783, according to principles pioneered by the great French bridge-builder, Jean Perronet, using arches which are semi-elliptical in form and a roadway which runs flat from bank to bank. The semi-ellipse is a most graceful shape, especially when mirrored in the water at high tide, and to my eye this is the most beautiful bridge in the County. The cutwaters are rounded in plan and roughly textured to contrast with the smooth-faced stone of the rest of the structure; they are surmounted by niches which pass right through the piers between the arches, lightening the structure both in appearance and in actual fact; and these niches are each capped by a pediment carried on Tuscan columns which stress the vertical and thus counteract the horizontal emphasis given to this long bridge by its cornice and balustrade. No wonder that Harrison won the first prize of twenty guineas and the commission to build the bridge, at a cost of £14,000.

Harrison launched the semi-elliptical arch on a long and successful career for major structures, although it was already used for canal bridges. Most of the more attractive masonry bridges in the County make use of it — from McAdam's New Lower Hodder Bridge of 1826 to the road bridge at the Crook o' Lune near Caton, which was built to the designs of Edward Paley in 1883. Between the Crook o' Lune and Skerton there are now four more bridges: a railway bridge, the road bridge at Halton built by the

Lancaster — Skerton Bridge

Midland Railway Company, the motorway bridge and the finest of them all, the Lune Aqueduct — but that brings us into the realm of Industrial Archaeology and thus of another chapter.

Chapter Six
The Architecture of the
Industrial Revolution

Darwen – India Mill Chimney

6. THE ARCHITECTURE OF
THE INDUSTRIAL REVOLUTION

Leaping boldly over the Lune on five wide semi-circular arches and carrying the canal sixty feet above the river, John Rennie's superb **aqueduct** a mile upstream of **Lancaster** is beyond question the finest masonry aqueduct in Britain. Ever since it opened in 1797, its scale and the sober magnificence of its rusticated stonework, its Doric pilasters and the deep frieze and cornice which they carry have made it a tourist attraction, and it is now regarded as one of the grandest monuments of the Industrial Revolution.

Good transport has always been important to industrial development. The Industrial Revolution – a shorthand term for a series of events which were the most important since Man discovered agriculture and which between, say, 1750 and 1850 completely transformed the economy and society first of this country and then of every country in the developed world – just could not have happened without the improvements to transport by road, by water and, lastly, by railway. Lancashire was one of the cradles of the Industrial Revolution, and more than

Lancaster – Lune Aqueduct

most Counties still has tangible reminders of that century-long upheaval which closed the door on a world of static, rural communities, a world based on natural materials and natural sources of power, and created the world in which we have grown up – of large towns, of factories and of power based on fossil fuels.

I have written at greater length on this fascinating subject in a booklet entitled 'Lancashire's Early Industrial Heritage' (also published by the County Council), so this chapter will merely concentrate on the most interesting and attractive remains of the early industries of cotton and coal and of the developments in transport which enabled them to flourish as never before – or since.

The Earl of Derby used to be called the uncrowned King of Lancashire, and his power was based on the social prestige and wealth which came in the seventeenth and eighteenth centuries from the ownership of large estates. In the nineteenth century the power of the landed gentry, as a group if not in every individual case, was increasingly, but not entirely, supplanted by the power of local mill-owners and mine-owners who, in competition with hundreds of their fellows, created a new aristocracy based on industrial wealth. With few exceptions these men were not so much inventors as entrepreneurs and managers. Without the inventions, however, they would have had little opportunity to exercise their enterprise and managerial skill, so it is appropriate to begin by looking briefly at some of the machines which underlay the Industrial Revolution.

Machines do not fascinate everyone but, if well presented, can arouse most people's interest. The most accessible display of eighteenth-century textile machinery, which made possible the production of cotton cloth at an industrial scale rather than by the members of a family for their own use, is at **Blackburn** in the **Lewis Textile Museum**. Here one can see first of all the traditional handloom, in which the shuttle carrying the weft had to be passed by hand from side to side through the longitudinal threads of the warp. Next comes John Kay's 'fly shuttle', patented in 1733, in which the shuttle was jerked from side to side of the loom by a spring – which doubled the speed of weaving so that eight or ten spinners were thereafter needed to keep one weaver supplied with yarn. These new looms could not be used to

their fullest extent, therefore, until a means had been found to increase the supply of yarn.

It took more than thirty years for the solution to be found. First a handloom weaver called James Hargreaves patented his 'spinning jenny' in 1764; this was a hand-driven machine which spun yarn on eight spindles simultaneously. Opposition from traditional spinners who saw their livelihood being threatened forced Hargreaves to leave his home at Stanhill (which is now the village post office) but the mechanisation of the cotton industry had begun. It was continued by Richard Arkwright who saw the disadvantages of the jenny; it needed considerable skill to work it and could not produce yarn continuously . His experiments in what is now called Arkwright House in Preston led to the invention in 1769 of a hand-powered machine which was simpler to operate and spun, in one continuous process, a yarn which was relatively fine and also strong enough to be used as the warp in a piece of cloth. Pure cotton fabrics were thereafter possible.

Blackburn – Spinning Jenny

Arkwright was more interested in full-time factory production than in the part-time use of machines in people's homes. He soon left Lancashire for Derbyshire where factories producing silk cloth already existed, and where he developed a larger water-powered spinning machine, known as the 'water-frame'. His machines were quite widely used in Lancashire, but the machine which became the basis of the County's cotton-spinning industry in the nineteenth century was the 'mule', which Samuel Crompton invented in 1779. It was similar in operation to Hargreave's jenny, in that it moved back and forth spinning the yarn and then winding it on to a spindle; but it could produce a finer and more consistent yarn than Arkwright's water-frame, and successive modifications increased the number of spindles from the original thirty to more than a thousand. The last machine on view at Blackburn is the power loom which gradually replaced the handloom after about 1820. It is seen against a photomontage of a weaving shed at the beginning of this century.

To watch machinery actually at work is more interesting than seeing even the best static displays, and this is now possible at two places in Lancashire — spinning at the County Council's Museum at Helmshore, and weaving at Queen Street Mill at Harle Syke near Burnley.

The **HELMSHORE TEXTILE MUSEUM** is a working museum based in two adjacent mills, Higher Mill and Whitaker's Mill. Higher Mill was built as a water-powered fulling mill in 1789 — and so is probably the oldest mill building in the County. It contains a superb 'breast-shot' water wheel (so called because the water strikes the wheel at a higher level than the axle) which can generate fifty horsepower. This will, it is hoped, be connected before long to drive the fulling-stocks, where lengths of woollen cloth were soaked in a sort of detergent and pounded with heavy hammers to make them shrink and thus tighten the weave. The Mill also contains a truly beautiful beam engine built in 1846. It has at one side a single

Helmshore — Water Wheel and Fulling Stocks (LCC Museums)

Helmshore – Mule Floor (LCC Museums)

vertical cylinder with a piston-rod attached to one end of a rocking beam, whose other end is attached to a crank in such a way that the up and down movement of the beam end is transformed into the rotary motion which will drive a piece of machinery. What is as beautiful as the elegant simplicity of the mechanics is the simple elegance of the machine itself. Every part is finely shaped – from the valve gear and other working parts which are enclosed within the panelled base to the six fluted cast-iron columns which carry the entablature-like framework supporting the beam.

The second, and probably more interesting, part of the Museum is in Whitaker's Mill, a formerly steam-powered mill which was rebuilt in 1860 after a fire. Here one can see not merely displays which outline the rise and fall of the Lancashire textile industry and its associated industries,

but also a full set of the machines which prepare and spin cotton yarn; and, by prior arrangement, an internationally important collection of early textile machines. These include an improved jenny and a later version of the water-frame which was originally installed at Arkwright's Mill at Cromford near Matlock. The climax to a visit is, however, the mule-floor where a member of the museum staff explains the process and works the eighty-year-old self-acting mules which, each time they roll back and forth, produce half a mile of a soft yarn suitable for such cloths as flannelette.

The continuation of the process can be seen no more than a dozen miles away at **Harle Syke,** where another working museum has been established by Burnley Borough Council in the **Queen Street Mill.** Here the emphasis is on the weaving branch of the industry which was concentrated more in

North East Lancashire. One can see the preparation of the warps and then under the north-lit roofs see the Lancashire looms at work, driven by line-shafts and belts to produce the traditional grey cloth; and one cannot fail to hear the deafening rhythmic clickety-clack, which forced the loom-minders to use sign language or to lipread.

In total contrast to this din is the source of the power which causes it, the five-hundred-horsepower steam engine itself which, for me, is the highlight of a visit. Built in 1895, it is unique since it is the only steam engine still to work in a Lancashire cotton weaving shed. It is what is called a 'tandem-compound' engine, in which steam which has used part of its energy at high pressure in a small cylinder is passed into a larger low-pressure cylinder placed immediately behind in such a way that the pistons in both cylinders drive the same piston rod. It sounds, and is, a complicated piece of machinery, but wonderful to watch in the smoothness of its working. It was renamed 'Peace' at the end of the First World War, but the name is very apt because the working of a mill engine is remarkably quiet; all one hears is the light click of the valve gear and the whirr of the flywheel turning at speed through the air.

The other major development in late nineteenth-century steam engines was the 'cross-compound' type, where the flywheel rotates between the high-pressure and low-pressure cylinders, and the steam travels across the machine rather than from front to back. Such an engine can be seen on the main road (A666) outside **India Mill** at **Darwen** and looks more impressive than a tandem-compound, which is more compact. Such a machine also looks more impressive at work, with its two piston rods — one comes out as the other slides back — to drive the single flywheel. Fortunately, one can still be seen at work at regular intervals in **Barnoldswick,** in the engine house of the now-demolished **Bancroft Shed.** It dates from 1922 and produced six hundred horsepower to drive the looms in what was the last weaving shed to be built in the present County of Lancashire (though it was then in Yorkshire). The shed was closed in 1978, but the engine has been preserved in working order and, like its cousin at Harle Syke, is well worth a visit.

As I wrote earlier, the late eighteenth-century Higher Mill at Helmshore was powered by water; but none of the later mills could have operated without coal. It was Lancashire's good fortune that it had

Darwen — Steam Engine

abundant supplies of coal to be exploited when they were most needed in the nineteenth century. The Lancaster Canal was begun in the late 1790s to carry coal from Wigan to Preston, Lancaster and, ultimately, to Kendal; and the Leeds and Liverpool Canal was diverted from its original route through Whalley and Leyland to pass through the Burnley area, where deep mining was developing. Another centre of mining was Chorley, but virtually nothing remains of all this activity in either town — for the opencast coal-mining west of Chorley is a post-war intrusion. The fall of King Coal was even more calamitous than that of King Cotton, and the only significant visible reminder of coal mining in Lancashire is now the little dock built in 1869 off the Leeds and Liverpool Canal to serve **Aspen Colliery, Oswaldtwistle.** Next to it stand three banks of 'bee hive' ovens where coal was burnt with a minimum of air to produce coke.

The remains of steam-powered mills built alongside canals can be seen at Blackburn, Chorley, and even at Lancaster. The best place to see them, though, is at **Burnley** in the so-called **Weavers' Triangle** between Manchester Road and Westgate. Most mills are utilitarian structures, built to house the machinery which could turn bales of cotton into gold sovereigns, and few offer much pleasure to anyone who is not interested in the development of methods of construction. Nevertheless, for precisely that reason they are important to the history of architecture (which involves plans and structures as well as façades and interior decoration) so, as far as I am concerned, the best of them count as part of Lancashire's heritage.

The oldest mill building in **Preston,** what used to be **Spital Moss Mill** off **Fylde Road,** was built in 1796. It is hardly attractive but is the only early mill now in the County to pay lipservice to the Classical tradition with its slightly projecting centre of three bays under a pediment. For the next fifty years most mills were to have no architectural pretensions whatsoever, but some of them have architectural distinction in the way that the tall-windowed engine houses are integrated with the rest of the buildings. There are two early canal-side mills at Lancaster on either side of Moor Lane; they were built around 1820, and have a slightly rugged attraction in their sloping walls and small-paned windows.

A similar, though larger, mill was built in 1835 at **Calder Vale.** It was originally

Oswaldtwistle – 'Beehive' Coke Ovens

powered by water from a reservoir still visible about a quarter-mile upstream and is a good example of the second generation of textile mill, where thick timber beams spanning considerable distances between masonry walls are supported by rows of cast-iron columns. (The first generation had been narrow structures crossed by unsupported timber beams). The columns at Calder Vale

Galgate Mills

cannot, however, be seen because the mill is still in operation; similar structures can be seen, though, at **Galgate** on either side of **Chapel Lane.** The stone-built mill of the 1830s and the brick-built mill, which dates from 1852, now house showrooms displaying second-hand furniture and new bathroom suites respectively. Both are part of a complex of mills founded in 1792 and originally powered by water to spin silk.

The brick building also includes the tall engine house which originally accommodated a beam engine, but neither this nor any of the machinery it once drove now remains. This latest mill building at Galgate is also interesting for displaying the pilasters at the corners which are typical of classically-inspired buildings of the 1830s and 1840s; it shows that by the middle of the nineteenth century some mill owners were taking thought about external appearances.

There are other good examples worth mentioning of this concern with façade design – at **India Mill** in **Darwen** which dates from 1867, at Brierfield Mill which is dated 1868 and at **Hardman's Mill, New Hall Hey** at **Rawtenstall** which was built in 1861 and is now the headquarters of the Rossendale Groundwork Trust, a body which involves local communities and local firms in the task of clearing industrial dereliction. The original owners of each of these large buildings were equally concerned to be up-to-date in their means of construction because, to the best of my knowledge, each of them is an example of the fourth generation of mill, where cast-iron columns carry cast-iron beams which then support shallow brick arches to create a structure which would be fireproof or at least prevent the spread of fire from floor to floor. (The third generation had merely had cast-iron columns and cast-iron beams supporting timber floors).

The fifth generation of mills was the last and can be recognised without difficulty from the size of their windows, and also from the fact that they are almost always faced with hard red bricks. These are often nicknamed 'Accrington bloods', although they were made – by machine and no longer by hand – in many other places in the coalmining areas. The windows of these mills are large because the outside walls no longer carry the main weight of the building, which was a self-supporting skeleton of steelwork needing no more than external cladding. By virtue of their size, these brick and glass leviathans are landmarks in their own right, like Tulketh Mill which dominates the northern skyline of

Rawtenstall – New Hall Hey Mill

Coppull – Ring Mill

Preston, or Imperial Mill in Blackburn whose copper-clad domes cannot be missed from the roundabouts at the end of the M65. My favourite is right at the southern end of Lancashire, the former **Ring Mill** at **Coppull** which, with its terracotta trimmings, dates from 1906. It is the first building of any size which one sees after crossing the County boundary in the train from London and is now being converted into offices and workshops as an immense act of faith in the future called the Coppull Enterprise Centre.

Several of the mill buildings which I have mentioned in the last few paragraphs – and this is one of the reasons I have chosen them rather than other examples – have fine chimneys. Early chimneys, like early mills, were utilitarian structures, usually square in shape, as at Galgate. Later in the nineteenth century, however, they were treated as important elements in the design of a mill and often, but not always, round on plan. When

every mill town presented a forest of smoking chimneys to the view, a particularly tall, slender or well-designed one was a source of pride and of good publicity.

The fullest and most concentrated collection of mill chimneys in the County is at **Burnley,** where the finest are the slender round one with a pronounced cornice at Newton Mill on Sutcliffe Street and the 'candlestick chimney' – with a round shaft on a square base – which rises above the mill on **Wiseman Street.** Both of them are in the Weavers' Triangle and can be seen well from the canal towpath to the west of Manchester Road Wharf. The two most striking chimneys in Lancashire are very different in character, though both date from the 1860s. The stone chimney at **New Hall Hey** in **Rawtenstall** has a slender, tapering square shaft with chamfered corners and a cornice surmounted by a cast-iron balustrade – a very elegant design. In complete contrast is the chimney at

96

India Mill, Darwen, which is taller and more robust, built of brick on a massive base of rock-faced stonework and detailed so as to look rather like the belltower of St. Mark's Cathedral in Venice, with windows at intervals and an elaborate double cornice towards the top: it is a sight which I find unforgettable rather than beautiful.

Weaving was the last of the textile processes to be fully mechanised. A power loom had been patented as early as 1785 by Edmund Cartwright, a Leicestershire clergyman, but another generation was to pass before it was developed into a machine which could be satisfactorily used in factories to increase productivity and reduce production costs. Thereafter handloom weaving declined, often in circumstances of great hardship and distress, but between 1790 and 1820 hundreds of houses were specially built to accommodate weavers and their families, who enjoyed a higher standard of living than most other craftsmen. These houses can often be recognised, because they stand out as taller than their neighbours. Among the best remaining examples are those around **West View Place** in **Blackburn,** which have cellar workshops, and in **Church Street** in **Ribchester** where a long terrace of houses dating from the 1790s survives with several workshops in the attics.

These houses in Ribchester are typical of East Lancashire, where woollen rather than cotton cloth was woven well into the nineteenth century, and weaving rooms tended to be in the drier upper storeys of houses, well lit by long ranges of windows. Many lights of these long windows have subsequently been blocked, but examples are to be found almost everywhere. Perhaps the most interesting are the so-called 'Weavers Cottages' at **Fall Barn Fold** in **Rawtenstall,** which are in fact a late eighteenth-century loomshop. This was a sort of early factory,

Rawtenstall — 'Weavers Cottages'

providing workspace for handloom weavers on two upper floors each lit by six south-facing triple windows, with (now demolished) living quarters at the rear. As such it offered a sort of halfway-house between domestic industry and factory production, in that weavers worked in company with others, rather than singly at home, but kept their status as skilled craftsmen rather than being machine minders.

Many of the early cotton mills were, as I wrote before, powered in the traditional way by water and were therefore built on sites where a waterfall with an adequate flow of water was available. Such places were as often as not at some distance from villages or even farmsteads, so that the more enlightened millowners in the early nineteenth century built small settlements near their mills to house at least their more important workers and thus ensure the presence of a skilled workforce. One of the prettiest of these villages is the nucleus of the present village of **Belmont** and was built to house some of the workers in the bleach and dye works, which were established in the nearby valley to use the pure waters of Eagley Brook. There are rows of early stone-roofed cottages along the main road and also on

some short streets to the east, including a row of fourteen called Maria Square with a datestone of 1804. A few miles nearer Preston along the same main road – the A675 – is the somewhat later **Abbey Village.** Originally in the 1840s this had about sixty cottages built for the workers of Abbey Mill, so called because Whalley Abbey had owned land in the area. The village was extended later in the nineteenth century, and for about a quarter of a mile in otherwise open countryside there is a sudden urban feel.

A village with a more rural feeling, probably because it is set, not in semi-moorland but in a steep-sided well-wooded valley, is **Calder Vale** which was begun in 1835 with housing for key workers in what is called Long Row and, later, in the Victoria and Albert Terraces. **Galgate** is another mill village with houses of different dates. Chapel Lane (where the mill stands) contains the oldest cottages, built of stone with two storeys, plus what used to be the village school; the houses on the main road to Lancaster are taller, brick-built and rendered, and probably date from the period of the mill's expansion in the mid-nineteenth century, when the coming of the railway brought coal and made the mill's water wheel redundant.

Abbey Village

98

Sunderland Point

After the middle of the nineteenth century all mills were designed to be steam-powered and tended to be built in the growing towns of the Lancashire coalfields and thus to reinforce this growth. Terrace after terrace of houses were built, hardly distinguishable from their neighbours and datable only by the minute details of their decoration and the names of some of the streets themselves, which range from battles like Alma to statesmen like Gladstone or Garibaldi. Some of the most attractive streets in any of the industrial towns are at Padiham where Gawthorpe Street and Albert Street may have been designed in the office of Sir Charles Barry. A late-developing mill village was Harle Syke, where the late nineteenth-century streets to the north of the churchyard of St. James' Church form a pleasing ensemble on the edge of open countryside which stretches away to the Pennine Moors. But Harle Syke is an exception and not the rule, and most of the houses in Lancashire's Victorian towns – like those in every other County in the country – are of greater interest to the social historian (like Nigel Morgan, who has written a fascinating book on housing in Victorian Preston) than to the average visitor. For that reason it is all the more pleasing to come across something like the Spring Vale Garden Village at Darwen, which was built in the early years of this century by the Quaker owners of the

neighbouring Greenfield Mill and has semi-detached cottages, built around a sort of village green.

As I wrote at the beginning of this chapter, the Industrial Revolution could not have occurred without the developments in transport which preceded and then accompanied it. At its simplest, the cotton industry could not have grown without ports through which to import its raw materials and export its finished products. Whatever the local legends say, none of the ports in the present County was ever as important as Liverpool, even before its great expansion in the eighteenth and, above all, nineteenth centuries. The earliest surviving remains of a port in Lancashire are at **Sunderland Point,** which was established soon after 1700 at the mouth of the Lune by a Lancaster merchant called Robert Lawson, who lived at Sunderland Hall. Feeling that the facilities in Lancaster itself were too poor, he built some warehouses and a small quay where goods could be unloaded for transport by cart to Lancaster, whenever the tide allowed this. Since it is on the north bank of the Lune, Sunderland was not, however, a very safe anchorage, and so another mooring was established on a less exposed site on the opposite bank near Glasson. Sunderland Point was superseded and has been virtually fossilised ever since, except for a brief period

99

in the early nineteenth century when it was a seaside resort. Only a few houses and Lawson's quay remain, with a single Georgian gatepier which stands like a monument to hopes which were never fulfilled.

The unloading arrangements at Glasson were soon found to be inadequate, so in 1749 the merchants of Lancaster persuaded Parliament to pass an Act which created the town's Port Commission; it still survives but its office is now at Glasson. The Commission built **St. George's Quay** in **Lancaster** just downstream from the (now demolished) Old Bridge; it also improved the channel in the Lune and charged tolls on ships and cargoes to pay for the work. Apart from the trees which line it, the Quay remains relatively unchanged to this day — a mixture of houses and taller, gaunt warehouses, some of which retain their old wooden cranes above the central loading slot. The finest building on the Quay is the former **Customs House** which was built in 1764, not merely for the mundane purpose of collecting money but also to be a symbol of the port's pride and aspirations. It was designed by the local architect, Robert Gillow, who studied Carr's plans for Lytham Hall and then produced an elegant Palladian façade with an Ionic portico, whose four columns are each shaped from a single block of the local sandstone. Gillow is in fact, and rightly, more famous as a furniture designer, and the best collections of his furniture are at the Judges' Lodgings in Lancaster and at Leighton Hall.

The Customs House now accommodates the City Council's fascinating **Maritime Museum,** which deals not merely with the history of the port of Lancaster and its links with the West Indies slave and sugar trade but also with the port of Heysham, the Lancaster Canal and the fishing industry in Morecambe Bay. An extension opened at the top of the neighbouring warehouse takes the story further, with displays on the ecology of

Lancaster — Maritime Museum

Morecambe Bay and on the gas-field which has recently started production. There are also full-scale mock-ups (with recorded readings from contemporary descriptions) of a late eighteenth-century coach crossing the Sands of Morecambe Bay and of the 'Waterwitch' canal packet, which sailed from Preston to Kendal in seven hours in the days before the railway.

Glasson Dock

The trade and prosperity of Lancaster's merchants grew – as can be seen in the Georgian houses which stand on several of the City's streets – but the port's facilities were unable to cope, so eventually in 1783 the Port Commission began to build a wet dock at **Glasson** behind the old quay. This enabled ocean-going ships, which could not or would not attempt the passage up the treacherous channel of the Lune, to pass through the lock gates at high tide and then to float upright all of the time. A link to the Lancaster Canal was made in 1826, so that small boats could travel directly to Lancaster and Kendal or to Preston, and for a generation more the port enjoyed a modest prosperity. Lancaster's foreign trade was, however, completely eclipsed by Liverpool's, and its coastal trade declined after the development of the docks at Fleetwood, Preston and Heysham. Glasson is now a village in Lancaster's commuter-belt, but the Dock with its tiny lighthouse is still a working port, and there is nearly always a small foreign coaster moored at the quayside to give a slightly exotic interest to the scene.

Fleetwood – Lower Lighthouse

The port of Preston has closed in recent years, and only the large expanse of the

Albert Edward Dock, where the 'SS Manxman' is moored, reminds us now of its former activity. Its decline was largely due to the fact that it was only accessible at high tide, when convoys of ships would steam up and down the narrow channel of the Ribble and give the surreal impression that they were sailing across open fields. Its role as the premier port of the County has therefore been assumed by **Fleetwood** which was developed in the 1840s by the then squire of Rossall Grange, Sir Peter Hesketh-Fleetwood. He dreamed of building on his estate at the mouth of the Wyre a port and seaside resort which would be accessible from everywhere by railway. Streets were laid out to the designs of the fashionable architect, Decimus Burton, who also designed the two **lighthouses** – the tall sandstone column called the Pharos in the town and the pretty little octagonal tower on its square colonnaded base by the shore; their gas lights, when lined up one above the other, were leading lights to guide ships' masters up the Wyre channel.

Burton was also the architect of the elegant North Euston Hotel, so called because after 1840 it was the northern terminus of the line from London and provided accommodation for people before the sea voyage to Ardrossan near Glasgow. Queen Victoria made the journey in the opposite direction in 1847, but the present main line over Shap Fell had been

101

opened in 1846, and Sir Peter's more roundabout and leisurely route was quickly superseded. His money ran out too; he had to sell his estate, and his house became the nucleus of Rossall School. The town thrived modestly as a seaside resort, enjoying (as it still does) fine views across Morecambe Bay to the Lakeland fells and also eastwards to the outliers of the Pennines. The port turned to general cargo and then to inshore and deep-sea fishing, reaching its peak just before and just after the Second World War when 75,000 tons of fish were landed each year. Since the decline of the fishing fleet, Fleetwood's main activity is the scheduled coming and going of the impressive but ugly roll-on roll-off ferries which link the town to ports on the other side of the Irish Sea. All this story and more is graphically told in the **Fleetwood Museum** on **Dock Street.** There are displays of nets and other tackle used for fishing salmon and shrimps in Morecambe Bay, and models of ships and trawls, as well as a mock up of the bridge of a trawler which, with photographs, evokes something of the hard work and hardships of the life of the deep-sea fishermen.

Fleetwood was the first port of the railway age, but ports preceded railways and needed good roads to their hinterlands, if they were to flourish. The roads north and south of Lancaster were improved by turnpike trusts established a couple of years after the Port Commission, and by 1760 turnpikes linked Preston and Burnley to all the other important towns in the County. At the end of the eighteenth century the system of turnpikes approximated to the present-day network of A roads. These new roads were not maintained by local authorities, as now, but by turnpike trusts whose officers were empowered to levy tolls on the various types of road users, according to a schedule which was painted on a board fixed outside each toll house. By far the best example now in Lancashire is at **Barrowford** where the **Toll House,** built in 1803, has been admirably restored by the Pendle Heritage Centre to contain a small museum. The toll board details the charges for such travellers as cattle and sheep as well as for vehicles; people with sharp eyes and a little patience will notice that waggons with wider wheels were charged less than those of a similar size with narrow wheels – because it was thought that they would do the turnpike company a good turn by rolling the surface of the road rather than cutting into it. There are other such toll

boards on display at the Rossendale Museum in Rawtenstall.

There are several other toll houses in the County – at Oaks Bar in Clayton-le-Dale and at Simonstone, for example – but the most interesting one is just north of **Garstang** where the B6430 joins the A6. It probably dates from the 1820s when parts of the road from Garstang to Lancaster were realigned: as one drives along the present A6, one crosses the old road which snakes from side to side. The **toll house** at Garstang, like most others, has been extended but is more than usually interesting because the posts for the tollgate (which was normally kept closed!) survive on either side of the road. The A6 north and south of Garstang also has the best series of turnpike milestones in the County, though there are interesting ones made of cast-iron on the A49 south of Bamber Bridge.

Barrowford – Toll House

There are two types: south of Garstang the stones are round-faced and are inset with cast-iron plates bearing mid-eighteenth century cursive lettering indicating the distances to Garstang and Preston; to the north the triangular stones placed on the newly aligned road have plates with fine Roman lettering. The sequence continues north of Lancaster as far as the County boundary south of Burton-in-Kendal.

There are a few milestones which antedate the turnpikes, and probably the earliest is just by the Hall at **Melling;** it has carved fingers to show the way to Kirkby Lonsdale or Bentham, but no distances. In those north-eastern parts of the present County which

Charnock Richard – Mile Post

The difference in the tolls displayed at Barrowford for vehicles with wider and narrower wheels is a reminder of the difficulties of maintaining firm road surfaces in the days before tarmacadam; and — consequently — of moving heavy goods around the country. As many as possible of them were therefore transported by water, around the coast, up river estuaries and then, from the later eighteenth century, on the growing system of canals which were built to link the major rivers in the country. Two centuries on, we are so used to regarding canals as places for pleasant walks or boating holidays that we tend to forget that they were the major arteries of commerce for a couple of generations. Canals were water turnpikes, built by private companies and open to all who would pay the tolls and thus contribute to the expense of building and maintenance. On the Lancaster side of the **Lune aqueduct** there are two lines of Latin verse, composed by the town's Roman Catholic priest in 1797, to celebrate the fact that things which had once been remote were now connected, and that rivers had been linked by the skill of men to create new sources of wealth. On the upstream side is a more laconic inscription in English and larger letters: TO PUBLIC PROSPERITY.

Canals were the greatest feats of civil engineering in their day, and a number of important monuments remain. You might think that they would be something of an anticlimax after the Lune aqueduct, but several more are worth seeing, including two which are easily accessible. Rennie's **aqueduct** at **Garstang** with its semi-elliptical arch over the Wyre is a masterpiece of restrained elegance, in which alternate bands of plain and rockfaced masonry emphasise horizontality and therefore suggest repose. On the other hand, the **aqueduct** which Robert Whitworth designed at **Ewood** in **Blackburn** soon after 1810 is very expressive — in the way that the apparent scale of the stones of the semi-circular arch is emphasised by the deeply incised radiating joints — of the effort involved in carrying the Leeds and Liverpool Canal over the road and the River Darwen.

Bridges carrying roads over canals are much more common; there are some 250 in the County, mostly built to roughly the same pattern (designed first by James Brindley in about 1760) with a semi-elliptical arch which gives eight feet of headroom above the water

used to be in Yorkshire, there are a number of milestones erected after an Order by the West Riding Magistrates in 1738. This stated that stones had to be placed at important junctions to show the distance to the nearest market towns. There is a good example dated 1766 near the **Higher Hodder Bridge,** but the best one is at **Dunsop Bridge**. It bears the date 1739 and also serves as the base for a nineteenth-century wrought-iron finger-post whose painted lettering is virtually illegible. There is a modern guide post standing right next to it, and, if one compares the present-day mileages with those of 1739, one notices that the older figures are lower: the reason is that the 'customary mile' used in 1739 was about forty per cent longer than our 'statutory mile', which was not standardised until Victorian times.

level and enough height over the towpath for a man and horse to walk underneath without discomfort. What I did not realise until recently (when a bridge near my house was repaired) is that what appear to be semi-elliptical arches are in fact elliptical tubes of masonry half-filled with water, because the stonework continues under the canal itself. The most interesting type of canal bridge is the roving bridge of which the best example in Lancashire is **Basin Bridge** in **Lancaster,** where the towpath changes from the west to the east bank of the canal so that through traffic would not interfere with barges unloading coal on the side of the canal basins off Aldcliffe Road. The idea is simplicity itself but, like all simple ideas, needed a person of genius to think of it first.

Lancaster – Basin Bridge

Look at the photograph and imagine a horse walking towards us on the further bank towing a barge on its way from Preston: as soon as it has passed under the bridge, it turns hard left, up and over the bridge, while the tow-rope goes slack as the barge continues under its own momentum; the horse then canters down the towpath on the nearer side, takes up the slack on the tow-rope and then plods on towards Kendal. Half a mile to the north another (now altered) roving bridge allows it to follow the towpath back to the west bank where it continues to the end of the canal at Kendal.

Walking on canal towpaths is one of the most agreeable ways of seeing the Lancashire countryside, because they are quiet, they are safe, and one can go at the speed one wants. A mile to the north of Lancaster one can cross the Lune with its pleasantly wooded banks and then come out on a winding stretch with fine views over Morecambe Bay to the Lakeland mountains. South of Lancaster one passes through the Deep Cutting, partly overhung with trees, and thereafter can walk for thirty miles to Preston with undulating Fylde farmland on the west and a backdrop of the smooth-faced fells of Bowland on the

Foulridge – Leeds and Liverpool Canal

Burnley – Manchester Road Wharf

east. The Leeds and Liverpool Canal offers an even greater variety of scenery. The earliest part to be built (in the 1770s) winds just above the drained marshlands of West Lancashire and then enters the deeply incised valley of the Douglas beyond Parbold; between Chorley and Blackburn it passes for the most part through an industrialised landscape, but beyond Blackburn industry gives way for several miles to open countryside, and one can enjoy occasional glimpses of the great whale-backed mass of Pendle Hill. In and beyond Burnley there is once more a succession of closed and open vistas, with industry on the east until Barrowford and the Foulridge tunnel. From here onwards there are extensive views over the Craven area towards the limestone sections of the Pennines, and then, after the locks at Greenber Field, it's downhill all the way to the North Sea.

Burnley is beyond compare the best place to see the most striking reminders of the impact of canals on towns. One can start at the **Manchester Road Wharf** which has recently been refurbished, and walk in either direction. The wharf itself was opened in 1796 as the temporary terminus of the canal from Leeds; it has therefore a toll house, which accommodates a small museum on Burnley and the Canal, as well as a warehouse. The earliest part of this was modelled on a contemporary barn, the nearest traditional building type, and then greatly extended with cranes and an overhanging canopy in the latter half of the nineteenth century. A ten minute walk to the west will take one through the so-called **Weavers' Triangle** area, through a landscape of now largely unoccupied nineteenth century mills whose chimneys are reflected in the canal. There is now no pall of smoke over

105

Burnley – Canal Embankment

the area and none of the muffled roar of clacking looms, but otherwise the scene is still evocative of Victorian times when Burnley was the cotton-weaving capital of the world.

A little further still – but less than a mile from the Manchester Road – one comes to the portal of the **Gannow Tunnel** whose stones are incised with what look like Egyptian hieroglyphs. I imagine that the mason involved had seen at a country house building site some stones carved with a form of rustication which is called 'vermiculation' (because it makes the stone look worm-eaten) and had decided to copy it here. One notices that the tunnel has no towpath through it – nor has the tunnel at Foulridge which is nearly a mile long! This meant that the bargees had to 'leg' their boats through, by lying on their sides on planks and, as it were, walking along the tunnel wall. It was dangerous and extremely tiring work, during which the more fortunate horses were led over the hill on the path which winds up to the right.

In the other direction from Manchester Road Wharf one comes to the other extreme of engineering and one of the wonders of the English canal system – the **embankment** which was completed in 1796 to carry the canal across the valley of the River Calder. The actual aqueduct is quite a small-scale affair, not much larger than a culvert, but the embankment is about three quarters of a mile long (though it is known locally as 'the 106

Straight Mile') and up to sixty feet high; no less than 300,000 cubic yards of material went into its construction. What is more, it is a superb vantage point – over the town of Burnley with its mills and its newly cleaned railway viaduct and then further to the hills on both sides, to Pendle on the west and, in the east, to Black Hameldon and Boulsworth Hill, which are part of the watershed of England beyond which lies Yorkshire.

It was intended, right from 1772 when the first plans for the Lancaster Canal were put forward, that it should join the Leeds and Liverpool at Eccleston west of Chorley. The link was not, however, made until 1816 – and then at Whittle-le-Woods to the north-east of Chorley; but the story is too long and complicated to tell here. There are other canal junctions in Lancashire, and the one at **Top Locks** near **Burscough** is probably the most interesting and attractive, so much so that it is the nucleus of a Conservation Area. The junction was made in 1781 to allow barges laden with coal to pass from Wigan down the Rufford Branch of the canal to Sollom, whence they could sail on tidal waters to Preston or Lancaster. Nothing of the all-consuming commercial drive which prompted the Liverpool committee to concentrate on the exploitation of the Wigan coalfield, rather than on the completion of the canal across the Pennines, is now evident except the very existence of the Rufford Branch. Top Locks is a peaceful little place with a couple of rows of cottages and a few passing pleasure craft. The dry dock which

Burscough – Top Locks

Johnson's Hillock Locks

the canal company built for the repair and maintenance of barges is still there, though, and often in use.

The link between the Lancaster and the Leeds and Liverpool was, as I wrote in the previous paragraph, finally completed in 1816. The canal from Leeds had been opened to Blackburn in 1810, but by this time the Lancaster Canal had been open to Wigan for nearly ten years; what is more, the other two trans-Pennine canals had been completed and the costs of the Leeds and Liverpool had risen to five times the original estimates made forty years previously. The directors were therefore forced to swallow their pride and had to accept that the best way of getting their canal from Blackburn to Wigan was to ask if it might join the Lancaster. The bargain was struck, and the long, pleasantly curving sequence of seven locks with pounds between them was built at **Johnson's Hillock** to allow the Leeds and Liverpool to drop sixty feet and thereafter use the Lancaster's route. Once more, there is no sign in these placid reed-banked waters of the financial worries and sleepless nights which preceded the decision. One might say, in conclusion, that the Leeds and Liverpool had the last word, because the Lancaster's route from Johnson's

Hillock to Preston via Walton Summit and then a tramway was closed many years ago, with the result that its line from Johnson's Hillock to Wigan is now regarded as part of the Leeds and Liverpool.

Canals enjoyed another generation of profitable trading before they began to be superseded by the railways, which then in their turn completed a full century of pre-eminence in the field of public transport. It is difficult for us to imagine the impact which the railways made in a still very rural England: they were built, largely by muscle power, at a rate which leaves our much-vaunted motorway system in the shade; and the steam-powered Iron Horse doubled speeds overnight and created an admiration, an affection and now a nostalgia greater than for any other product of the Industrial Revolution. All of these can be enjoyed to the full at **Carnforth,** a town which developed rapidly a century ago when its station was an important junction served by trains from three companies. One of the companies was the Furness Railway whose pretty stone-built signal box still stands at the end of the up platform on the Barrow line. From there it is but a long stone's throw to the Midland Railway's rebuilt brick and timber-framed signal box from Selside in 'Steamtown', which has put the name of Carnforth into the mouth of every railway enthusiast in the country.

Steamtown was established in the twenty-six acres of the locomotive depot which was the last one built, in 1944, by the London, Midland and Scottish Railway and, when it closed in 1968, was the last operational steam shed on British Railways — the home of the locomotive 'Oliver Cromwell', which in August of that year hauled what was thought to be the last scheduled steam passenger train over British Railway's metals. The depot is now Lancashire's third working museum, complete with its offices and workshops (which are still in use), its water columns and the vacuum-operated turntable and, towering above them all, the ugly concrete bulk of the locomotive coaling plant which is now unique in Britain. In addition, Steamtown is the home of about thirty steam locomotives, including 'Flying Scotsman', 'Lord Nelson' and the streamlined 'Sir Nigel Gresley', plus a couple from the Continent. All of these have been restored to working order and pull trains at weekends on a short

stretch of line at Carnforth, or work across to York or around the Cumbrian Coast. There are also various items of old rolling stock, a model railway and a narrow-gauge steam train which runs daily during July and August.

The beginning of the Railway Age is conventionally placed in the year 1830, when the Liverpool and Manchester Railway — both towns were then in Lancashire — began its scheduled steam-hauled services for both goods and passengers. The success of the line stimulated other companies to build railways which would connect with it or link it to London. Both aims were achieved when the first train arrived in **Preston** in 1838, running over the five wide-spanned, semi-elliptical arches of the North Union Railway Company's **Ribble Viaduct,** designed by Charles Vignoles. It can best be seen from Miller Park; imagine it without the later widenings upstream and downstream, and it must have been a structure of considerable elegance and daring.

Victorian railway engineers continued from the point reached by fifty years of canal

Carnforth — Steamtown

building and were no longer daunted by the prospect of building lines through hills and across valleys, as the network of lines spread from Preston and Manchester to the growing industrial towns of East Lancashire. Railways always took a more direct route than did canals, and this can best be seen at Capernwray, near Carnforth, where the railway and the canal cross the River Keer. The canal made a longish détour upstream in 1797 to a narrow-arched stone aqueduct, whereas the railway, which was opened in 1850, went straight across the river on a tall viaduct flanked by embankments; incidentally, at the foot of the viaduct is a low packhorse bridge. The longest tunnel in Lancashire — a little over a mile — is at Sough on the Bolton to Blackburn line, but what one can see is not worth the trouble of finding it. Much shorter but equally impressive as a symbol of the determination of Victorian railway companies and their engineers in the pursuit of business and profit are the two

Newchurch Tunnels at **Waterfoot,** which were built first in 1851 and then in 1881 to take the line from Rawtenstall to Bacup through the narrowest part of the rocky Irwell Gorge.

It is always easier to appreciate the daring of the engineers and the skill and courage of the builders when one is looking at viaducts rather than tunnels, and there are several fine ones to visit in Lancashire. The most attractive one is probably the little viaduct at **Preston,** built in 1840 over **Fylde Road** to carry the line to Lancaster: it looks like a small-scale triumphal arch. The most striking viaducts are, as one would expect, in the hills of East Lancashire. The tallest is at **Healey Dell** in **Whitworth** and was built in 1870 with eight narrow arches to carry the Rochdale to Facit line one hundred and twelve feet above the River Spodden; it now carries a footpath through part of the Healey Dell nature reserve.

Whalley Viaduct

Preston Station

I have already mentioned the viaduct at **Burnley** which strides across the valley of the Calder to the west of the town centre; the one at **Accrington,** which also dates from 1848, is closer to the centre as it runs on a slight curve over the River Hyndburn and so it dominates most views in the town with some of its nineteen arches. But the most impressive of all is **Whalley Viaduct** which was completed in 1850 using forty-eight arches built of seven million bricks to carry the Blackburn to Clitheroe line sixty-five feet above the Calder. With a length of about seven hundred yards it is a major landscape feature, visible for miles around, but, where it crosses the lane leading to the Abbey ruins, its designer made it pay a sort of homage to the nearby medieval gatehouse by giving Gothic details to the flanking arches.

Preston had the earliest major station in the present County and soon became the centre of a network of lines radiating in six directions. For a long time most of these lines had separate termini, but in 1880 all but one of them were amalgamated into a single complex which is still the present **station.** The newly built entrance on Butler Street lacks the slight grandeur of the original entrance off Fishergate, but does have the advantage of bringing one into the station at the level of the decorated steel roof trusses, so that one can look down as it were from the 'gods' onto the three island-platforms under the triple-aisled glazed train shed. The only other station which can compare with Preston's is at **Blackburn;** it was completed in 1888, with an impressive two-storey red brick office block, and has platforms at a high level under twin roofs supported on the outer walls.

Neither of **Lancaster's** stations can compete with this High Victorian confidence, but they are not without their interest. What is now the Nurses' Home opposite the Royal Infirmary was built as the town's first station in 1840 and was the terminus of the line from Preston. Standing at the top end of Penny Street, it looked down on what was then a largely Georgian town, so, since nobody really knew what a station

111

should look like, its two-storey façade was designed to look like the house of a contemporary gentleman, with a small pediment and a porch with Ionic capitals. When, however, the line from Preston was continued over Shap Fell to Carlisle in 1846, the original station became redundant, and the nucleus of the present **station** was built on the west side of the lines opposite the Castle. It too was designed as a house, in a scaled-up version of the standard stations on the Lancaster-Carlisle line - no longer in a Classical uniform but, with twin gables and large mullioned windows, looking rather like an Elizabethan manor house or, indeed, like the new Vicarage at Lancaster which was built in the same year.

The six years between Lancaster's two stations marked a watershed in the taste of the nineteenth century, a turning point in what has been called 'the Battle of the Styles' in which architects debated, and occasionally argued with great ferocity, about the way in which buildings should be designed. When Lancaster station was extended in 1858, the

Lancaster Station

office block was designed to complement the castle by looking like a keep with battlements and a watchtower. It was a clear sign that the advocates of the Gothic Revival had won, but I must not anticipate the subject of the next chapter.

Chapter Seven
The Battle of the Styles

Scarisbrick Hall

7. THE BATTLE OF THE STYLES

The revival of decorative motifs from the Middle Ages — which will suffice as a definition, if not as an explanation, of the Gothic Revival — had in fact begun in Lancashire nearly a hundred years before **Lancaster** station was built — and about a hundred yards from it, at the **Priory Church.**

Lancaster Priory — Tower

The tall tower, which composes so well with the body of the church and forms the climax of the view of the castle and church on their hill, was not built in medieval times, but was a replacement of an older tower (which had stood a few yards to the north) and was constructed to the designs of a Liverpool architect, Henry Sephton, between 1753 and 1755. The mere age of a building is not very important in my scale of values: it is not without interest, of course, that the Mother Church of the County Town should include the oldest example of the Gothic Revival in Lancashire, but it is of more significance to the County's heritage that it is a fine and striking tower, carefully designed to fit the scale and feel of the rest of the church, while only declaring its age (or its relative youth) in some of its details, like the angels' heads and little drops of leaves and the 'Chinese Chippendale' transom on the belfry openings.

Medieval details were seldom used in the eighteenth century, because Taste tended towards the copying of motifs known to the Romans, whose literature was the staple of every gentleman's education and whose ideas therefore underlay many of the prejudices of the age — to such an extent that, as we have seen in Chapter 2, it was not felt to be incongruous, in the monument to Sybill Wilson in Lancaster Priory, to represent a former Colonel in a Guards regiment in the uniform of a Roman soldier. Nevertheless, there was no rooted objection to 'Gothick' design, if for some reason it was thought appropriate. Sir Christopher Wren had completed Cardinal Wolsey's Tom Tower at Christ Church College, Oxford, in 1682 'to agree with the Founder's work' (as he put it); and his pupil Nicholas Hawksmoor designed the towers of Westminster Abbey in 1734 to complement the great fifteenth-century west window for much the same reason. Henry Sephton accepted this gentlemanly pattern of courtesy, and so too did Thomas Harrison (whose Skerton Bridge and St. John's Church I mentioned two chapters ago) when he accepted the commission to design the **Shire Hall** at **Lancaster Castle** in 1786.

Thomas Harrison had trained in Rome and would have preferred to design in the Classical manner, as he had begun to do for a similar commission at Chester Castle which is (dare I say it?) the finest complex of Georgian public buildings in the North of England. The presence at Lancaster Castle of the massive medieval keep, sundry towers and John of Gaunt's Gateway, along with the Priory Church a few yards away in the other direction, persuaded him, however, that it was appropriate to design the Shire Hall and the other court and prison buildings which are associated with it in the Gothic idiom. He chose as his model the latest of the Gothic styles — known to us now, but not in Harrison's day, as the Perpendicular style — with its large windows and panels of tracery; and, having accepted these constraints, he produced a masterpiece which, externally, composes well with the keep in an interplay of simple geometric masses and, internally, provides a series of interesting rooms and one splendid one.

The Shire Hall complex contains a court, which is directly linked to the prison and therefore still used for criminal cases where security is important. The Shire Hall itself is the first room which visitors to the Castle see, before going downstairs to the basement of the medieval Hadrian's Tower with its prison museum, to the 'dungeons' where the cells can be plunged into absolute darkness by the guide and finally to the 'drop-room'; this is where – until 1865 – prisoners who had been condemned to hang were brought, before they stepped out onto the specially built scaffold in front of the crowds who had flocked to the churchyard to watch them drop and die in public. More people were condemned to death at Lancaster Assizes than at any other Court in the country, but the Shire Hall was not associated with this licensed barbarity, because it was a court for civil cases. It is now the Castle's most beautiful room, hung with hundreds of shields bearing the arms of the Kings of England, the Constables of the Castle and the High Sheriffs of the County Palatine from the time of Richard I.

It is indeed a most impressive display, an encyclopaedia both of heraldry and of the County's history; but do not allow yourself to be side-tracked, for the Shire Hall is a beautiful room to be enjoyed in its own right. Built between 1796 and 1798, it is in fact a Gothic version of the Shire Hall which Harrison was designing at the same time in Chester. Whereas at Chester a domed ceiling rises from an entablature carried by a semi-circular ring of Ionic columns, at Lancaster a half-circle of Gothic pillars carry not merely the arches which support the panelled vault over the main part of the court room but also the arches of the vault over the surrounding aisle; it is a most ingenious and beautiful solution, giving easy public access to the court room while allowing the business of the court to proceed in suitably dignified surroundings. The stage, as it were, where all the high court-room drama was enacted – the bench for the judges and their clerks and the docks for the plaintiff and the defendant – is placed under a high panelled arch which spans the diameter of the room. All the furnishings in the room (and, indeed, in most of the building) were supplied in dark-painted woodwork by Gillows.

Behind the stage the character of the work changes abruptly from the bold skeletal structure of the Hall itself to the over-pretty

decoration of the series of panelled canopies which were added in the early 1800s to the designs of Joseph Gandy. To cut a long and sad story short, Harrison, who was something of a perfectionist, was trying to design and supervise two major projects at once, the Shire Hall complexes at Chester and at Lancaster. Since 1793 he had lived in Chester (which was a full day's journey away from Lancaster) and was accused by the Lancashire authorities of giving inadequate attention to their project. They were probably right; relations became strained, and in 1799, since

Lancaster Shire Hall
(LCC Property Services)

the bulk of the work was complete and funds were short, Harrison was asked to resign. Some years later, when money became available during a lull in the Napoleonic wars, the interior decoration of the courts and the rest of the prison buildings were completed by the less talented Gandy.

By the time that Harrison relinquished his work in Lancaster, many if not all architects were able and willing to design in 'Gothick' or 'Grecian' or any other style that was required of them. The archaeological discoveries, at which I hinted while writing about Lytham Hall in Chapter 4, had continued by then for half a century and showed, for example, that Roman architecture had been much more varied than people believed. A good deal was known too about the decorative motifs used at various times not merely in Greece and Italy, but also in the Middle East and as far away as India and China. Pattern books existed, and any architect worth his salt could turn his hand to any style. As knowledge of the decorative styles and constructional techniques of past cultures increased, and as the experience of engineers using materials like cast and wrought iron in new ways to create daring structures made them bolder, architects and architectural critics began to wonder what the style of the nineteenth century should be. The answer had been fairly clear in the eighteenth century — though I am sure that it is clearer to us with two hundred years of hindsight: a social and intellectual élite had decreed that in almost every case architecture should follow some form of Classical precedent.

But times were changing; the landed gentry were no longer the undisputed masters of the country, and many of the old certainties had been shaken, in part by the discoveries of archaeology and in part through political events like the French Revolution. James Richards (in his **National Trust Book of English Architecture** which is, I think, the best one-volume introduction to the subject) has placed the nineteenth century at the beginning of what he calls 'the Age of Confusion'. That name is a good one, but I have used a more traditional nickname for the title of this chapter, because the confusion arose later from the debates and disputes about what the appropriate style for the nineteenth century was.

The question never received a final answer; the architectural press reported the controversy which, of course, generated more heat than light. If anyone had the last word, it was perhaps Augustus Pugin, who stated categorically in the year 1836 that the Gothic style was the only appropriate one for use in a Christian country. But his word was law only during the middle third of the century; before and after that, practice differed and confusion reigned.

At the risk of being accused of over-simplification, I think that the confusion can be reduced somewhat by dividing the nineteenth century into three roughly equal periods, with turning points around the years 1840 and 1870 and then by looking at the bewildering mass of facts and buildings in terms of the rise and fall of the Gothic Revival. Almost every building of consequence in the middle third of the century was designed with details, and often with a structure, firmly based on medieval precedents; after that period the Middle Ages lost their posthumous grip on architectural practice; before the age of Pugin's intellectual ascendancy the medieval styles were used, but only when it was thought appropriate to do so. It is worth making this effort to understand the architecture of what one may loosely call Victorian England, because its very confusion makes it interesting and also because a good third of the finest buildings in the County were built during the nineteenth century.

While writing about aqueducts, mills and railway stations, I mentioned that Classical details were used on utilitarian buildings until well into the nineteenth century. The same was true of country houses, but none which is worth seeing is open to the public — with the exception of the rooms in Towneley Hall and Browsholme Hall which were mentioned at the end of Chapter 4. This is unfortunate, but my purpose is not to write a history of architecture in Lancashire; it is merely to try to explain the origins and significance of the most beautiful and interesting buildings which can be seen without difficulty.

The only buildings from the first third of the nineteenth century which are worth going any distance to see are — with one exception — churches, and most of these are Anglican ones too. The reason for this last fact is largely financial. Architectural quality does not depend entirely on money, as many over-elaborately decorated Victorian buildings prove, but it is difficult to create a building of quality if cheapness of first cost is the primary consideration. The majority of early Nonconformist chapels were primarily rooms in which worship could be offered and sermons heard; they were not aids to worship which sought to declare the glory of God in the form of the building itself. They tended therefore to be utilitarian in their outward appearance, and this is also true of Roman Catholic churches, which did not want to draw attention to themselves, although they did emphasise the importance of the altar by architectural richness within.

To Anglican eyes in the early nineteenth century both the Roman Catholics and the Methodists posed something of a threat, the former by surviving the less than total persecution in the seventeenth and eighteenth centuries, and the latter by making many converts among 'the labouring poor' (as people then said) by the bold assertion that, despite appearances, God loved all individuals equally, regardless of their social position. The Tory government of Lord Liverpool therefore had Acts of Parliament passed in 1818 and 1824 which encouraged the building of Anglican churches in the new industrial towns and in the industrial suburbs of older towns, by establishing a Commission with one and a half million pounds to spend in grant aid. Nearly ten per cent of the 214 so-called 'Commissioners' Churches' which were consequently built are to be found in the present County of Lancashire; if one makes the calculation in terms of the traditional County, the proportion rises to more than a third.

Very few of these churches are now open. The majority of them are fairly plain, but recognisable as Commissioners' Churches by their tall lancet windows, their gabled buttresses and generally insubstantial air: they look as though they were made of icing sugar rather than stone. A good example is St. Paul's on the Preston Ringway which was recently cleaned and converted to be the office and studios of Red Rose Radio. A more attractive example, in **Preston, St. Peter's Church** on **Fylde Road,** is also more accessible: it has been converted into the Arts Centre of Lancashire Polytechnic, and so one has an exhibition as well as a church to see. It was finished in 1825 and looks more like a traditional, that is, a pre-Reformation, church with a nave and aisles and a chancel which is more than just a shallow recess. Its

prettiest feature is also its most unusual one, and that is the delicate cast-iron arcade carrying the galleries — to maximise the seating capacity of the church — which are neatly set back behind the arches of the nave. The elaborate window tracery is also of cast iron, for the church's architect, Thomas Rickman, was not merely a scholar, to whom we owe the traditional terms — Early English, Decorated and Perpendicular — to describe the three major stylistic subdivisions of Gothic architecture, but was also interested in the use of 'modern' materials in building. The church was originally built with a bellcote which still survives on the western gable, but a tower was added in 1852 to the designs of Joseph Mitchell. Its slender spire, supported by four little flying buttresses and probably modelled on the spire at Kirkham which I shall mention in a moment, is the most attractive feature of the church.

Preston — St. Peter's Church

Probably the finest of the Commissioners' Churches in Lancashire is **St. George's** at **Chorley.** It dominates the town centre more than the old parish church of St. Leonard, which is in fact largely a Victorian reconstruction. St. George's was also built to the designs of Rickman and finished in 1825, but at £12,387 it cost nearly twice as much as the others I have mentioned. It is an impressive church, both outside and in, with a tall western tower whose belfry stage has three lancets of which only the central one is pierced. This motif of lancets is used consistently around the whole church, and the east window is composed of five lancets arranged in a stepped fashion. Inside, under a slightly spindly hammer beam roof, the two-centred arches, which run from west to east without any break between the nave and the chancel, are richly moulded and carried on clustered pillars. The galleries over the aisles are supported on the same sort of cast-iron columns and cusped arches as at St. Peter's in Preston.

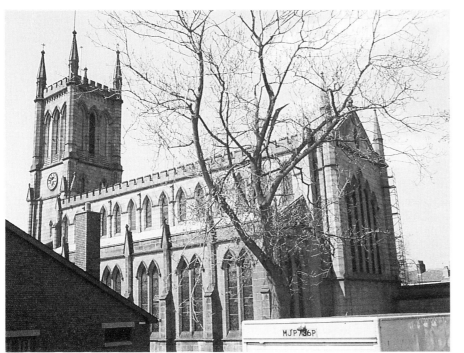

Chorley – St. George's Church

What in many ways is my favourite among the Commissioners' Churches in Lancashire is a much simpler building, **Holy Trinity** on **Accrington Road, Burnley.** Its façades appear much more solid than is normally the case and have a pleasing depth of modelling, with projecting buttresses along the sides and clasping buttresses at the corners of the tower; the paired lancets in the aisle walls are repeated in the bell openings. Altogether it is an impressively satisfying church, designed in 1835 by the little-known Lewis Vulliamy and built at the surprisingly low cost of just under £3,000. It stands above the complex of roundabouts leading to the M65, and my eyes are always drawn to it when I am driving in the area.

Not every Anglican church built in the 1820s and 1830s was a Commissioners' Church; some were rebuildings of old parish churches like **St. Mary's** at **Clitheroe** whose spire is a landmark at the other end of the town's main street from the castle. It too was

Burnley – Holy Trinity Church

designed by Rickman and is, externally, typical of its date with its tall windows and short chancel. Inside it is finer and more interesting, with tall arcades to divide the nave from the aisles and a fine hammer beam roof. As one would expect, there are galleries over the aisles, but they are set back behind the arcades and do not detract from the stately lines of the church.

A much plainer church whose nave was rebuilt on the old foundations is **St. Michael's, Kirkham,** designed by the Preston architect, Robert Roper. Outside, it has the lancets typical of its date; the inside follows the pattern of Poulton-le-Fylde's parish church with its impressively wide unaisled space under a panelled ceiling which appears to be supported by a series of shallow wooden arches. To the west is a gallery – there used to be three until a few years ago – with Gothic panelling. There are other items from the old church, like the brass chandelier (whose splendid curly supports are, however, recent) and some monuments to the Cliftons of Lytham Hall who, though they were Roman Catholics, were the lay rectors of Kirkham and drew a sizeable annual income from the tithes. The best feature of the church is, however, the tower and spire which were added at the west end in 1844 to the designs of the Lancaster architect, Edmund Sharpe, who had been a pupil of Thomas Rickman. It is one of the finest steeples in the County,

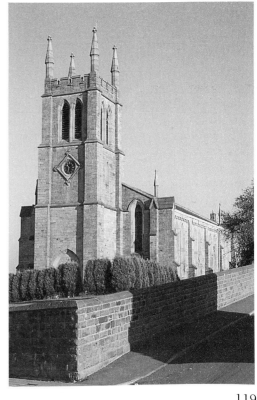

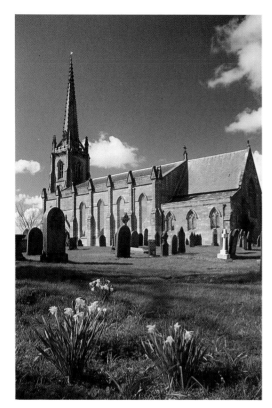

with deeply moulded buttresses at the corners of the tower, decorative details which become progressively richer as the height of the tower increases, and a recessed octagonal spire supported by small flying buttresses and decorated up each of its angles with little crockets.

Probably the most visited – and deservedly so – of these early nineteenth-century churches is **St. Mary's, Blackburn** which stands quietly in a large churchyard and is now the **Cathedral** of the Anglican diocese, founded in 1926. I shall mention in the next chapter the eastern extensions designed to make it more worthy of its higher status. The original church was built in 1826 to the designs of the Manchester architect, John Palmer, who was a Roman Catholic, but after it was damaged in a fire in 1831 Palmer consulted Rickman. They designed a church which is perhaps finer than any other Anglican church of the time, with a tall west tower, tall three-light windows in the aisles, and a very spacious, well-lit interior. The pillars in the nave are round with attached shafts and carry richly moulded arches, with a gilded cresting below the clearstorey windows. The many-ribbed vault with its finely carved bosses at the intersections of the ribs is especially attractive.

Palmer knew almost as much about medieval architecture as did Rickman and put what he knew into practice almost as

soon as Rickman did. His most famous church, which deserves to be better known, is the Roman Catholic church in **Pleasington;** it is dedicated to **St. Mary** and **St. John the Baptist.** It was built between 1816 and 1819 as a thank-offering by the local squire, John Butler, and this perhaps explains the boldness of the architectural statement a full ten years before the Catholic Emancipation Act allowed (rather than tolerated) the building of Catholic churches.

At first sight Palmer's church looks rather like a Commissioners' Church, but one soon notices that the details are different. To use Rickman's terminology, the clearstorey windows are Early English, simple lancets arranged in groups of three; the windows of the chancel are Decorated with richly flowing tracery patterns, while most of those in the aisles are Perpendicular, with a more ordered panel of tracery at the top and mullions which run straight up to the head of the arch. Palmer's avowed intent was to introduce into the building 'the different styles of architecture that prevailed in the

Kirkham – St. Michael's Church

Blackburn Cathedral

Pleasington Catholic Church

Not all Anglican churches were built in a form of the Gothic style; there was a — fortunately — short-lived fashion in the 1830s for churches designed to look as though they had been built in the twelfth century. There are half a dozen stone-built ones in and around Preston, as well as others of brick at Out Rawcliffe and Freckleton. They differ little in their general shape — only in their decorative details — from most Commissioners' churches. The strangest of them all is St. Mary's, off New Hall Lane in Preston; this has an unusual arrangement of western transepts and a weird tower, which is crowned by a spire like a witch's hat. A much more pleasing church, designed in 1837 by the same little-known Preston architect, John Latham, is **St. Thomas'** on **Lancaster Road, Preston.** It looks as though it has been transplanted from the South West of France, with its plainly decorated nave and aisles, shallow apse and, between them both, a tall but sturdy tower capped with an octagonal spire. The inside is disappointing and, in any case, being converted to a community centre, but the exterior is very pleasingly sculptural in its play of simple geometric shapes. I see it whenever I drive to work in Preston, and it always gives me pleasure.

While Anglicans and Roman Catholics were locked into a sort of rivalry about which denomination could produce the most striking church in the Gothic style,

kingdom from the days of King Ethelbert down to Henry VIII'. Needless to say, he failed, but the attempt is worthy of applause. The west doorway is modelled on the doorway of the chapter house at Whalley Abbey; the rose window above it would grace any French cathedral; the arch between them is decorated with dog-tooth moulding, which is also prominent inside in the decoration of both the tall arcades and also the clearstorey windows. The whole building is vaulted in lath and plaster, with medallions showing scenes from the life of Christ above the central aisle; there are also striking bas-reliefs showing St. Mary Magdalene and the Beheading of St. John the Baptist, on either side of the altar.

Another attractive Roman Catholic church, although like its Anglican contemporaries it suffers from an apparent lack of solidity, both inside and out, is **St. Ignatius'** at **Preston** which was built with a tower and a spire between 1833 and 1836, that is, shortly after the Catholic Emancipation Act. This spire was the first to be built by Roman Catholics in the County since the Reformation — only eight years after the one at the Anglican parish church of St. Mary at Mellor. It was therefore perhaps meant as a challenge to Anglican supremacy; it certainly provoked a reaction, which stimulated a rivalry, and the following twenty years or so saw the finest spires in the County being built. I have already mentioned the one at Kirkham.

Preston – St. Thomas' Church

Nonconformists refused to conform to this emulation and preferred until well after the middle of the century to use one of the Classical orders to clothe their chapels. It is rare to find one open except on a Sunday, when one can see that the traditional pattern of the interior with galleries around all four sides still survives in many cases, but the exteriors of these chapels are often very fine and obviously just as much designed to advertise the presence (and pretensions) of this or that congregation as any Anglican or Catholic steeple. Two of the best of such chapels are in **Rawtenstall** and provide an interesting contrast in the appearance and the 'feel' of the two major Classical orders used in chapels, the Ionic and the Corinthian

The **Longholme Methodist Church** on **Bacup Road** was the first to be built, in 1842, with a beautifully chaste two-storey exterior with pilasters at the corners and a pedimented portico of four unfluted Ionic columns. Part of the cost was borne by the Whitehead family who owned a neighbouring mill. A dozen or so years later the congregation was split by disagreements, and the Whiteheads withdrew their support from Longholme and contributed towards the cost of another chapel, which is now the **Old People's Centre** on **Haslingden Road**, overlooking the big roundabout. This is a much more assertive design, again two-storeyed, but everything is more heavily moulded, not least the portico with its pediment and large Corinthian capitals with their sumptuous display of acanthus leaves. In fact, most of the Nonconformist chapels of the third quarter of the century used the Corinthian order, and one of the most striking examples is the **Central Methodist Church** in **Lune Street, Preston** whose portico was remodelled in 1862 with a giant arch carried on paired columns. I cannot help finding it ironic that Nonconformist chapels, in their desire not to appear Anglican, should have espoused the Baroque forms used by the triumphant Catholic Church after the Counter-Reformation; but, once having chosen to go classical rather than gothic, they were carried along by the taste of the age which, as the century progressed, preferred more sumptuous details and more richly moulded textures in its buildings, whatever the style.

I shall return to this point in a few pages' time but let us first go back to the 1820s and the most attractive country house of the early Gothic Revival – **Leighton Hall.** Do your

best to visit this on a fine afternoon when the air is clear rather than hazy, because the view as one turns from the road into the drive across the park can be one of pure delight. The house is built of a very white limestone and sits in a half-saucer of tree-framed pasture land, backed by the Furness Fells. There are other outside attractions as well, for the bird lover or photographer, since on every fine day the hawks and falcons from the Leighton collection – many of whom have been rescued and brought back to health after accidents – put on a remarkable flying display.

Rawtenstall
– Longholme Methodist Church

Rawtenstall – Old People's Centre

Leighton Hall   The house itself appears to be substantially of the early nineteenth century, but is in fact both older and more recent; the rear wing, for example, probably goes back to the seventeenth century. The owners of Leighton have always been Roman Catholics, and during the 1745 rebellion the house was damaged by government troops, so George Towneley – a relative of the Towneleys of Towneley Hall – decided to rebuild it. The carcase of this Georgian house underlies most of what one now sees and can be glimpsed in the stable yard to the right behind the pretty Gothic disguise (which is similar to the work at Thurnham Hall, south of Lancaster); this was applied probably after 1822 when the house and estate were purchased by Richard Gillow. He was the son of the furniture designer and had sold the family business, in what would now be called a management buy-out, and retired to live the life of a country gentleman. His portrait in the entrance hall suggests that he was not displeased by his change of lifestyle. The final stage in the Gothicking of Leighton Hall came in 1870, when the Lancaster architects, Paley and Austin, added the tower and the cross-wing on the left, which create a very

picturesque design of controlled asymmetry – with height and bulk played off against length.

All this Gothic work is more than skin-deep, for several of the rooms are decorated in a Gothic manner. The Entrance Hall is perhaps the most beautiful room in the house. It has a screen of three shallow cast-iron arches on cast-iron clustered columns which separate the hall from the gracefully sweeping stone staircase. This is cantilevered out from the wall and its balusters are miniature versions of the columns of the screen. The house is still lived in by Richard Gillow's descendants, and you may well be shown around by the owner's wife, who clearly enjoys the task.

To the right of the Hall is the Dining Room, a darkly panelled room with windows like those of the Shire Hall in Lancaster. It is top-lit as well, because it was originally used as a billiard room – the Gillows were famous for their tables. I find the most attractive feature of this room the seven panels painted with Romantic landscapes but, as in every room in the house, there are also good pieces

Leighton Hall – Hall

of Gillow furniture, notably the sideboard supported by two one-legged birds and the expanding dining table which was patented in 1800 by the elder Richard Gillow. The Drawing Room, which has a much more Victorian feel to it thanks to the large bay window added by Paley and Austin, contains a beautifully veneered games table and a display table whose front is inlaid with exquisite sprays of flowers and foliage, both of late eighteenth-century date. There is, as I mentioned in Chapter 4, a good collection of later Gillow furniture in the Judges' Lodgings museum at Lancaster.

At the beginning of this chapter I remarked that the man whose mind dominated the thought and practice of architects in the middle decades of the nineteenth century was Augustus Pugin. He designed only one church in Lancashire, the Roman Catholic Church of St. John the Evangelist at Kirkham, which was opened for worship in 1845. It composes pleasingly enough from the south east, but the interior offers nothing special, and the spire is outclassed by Sharpe's spire at the Anglican church which I mentioned a few pages ago. Pugin's importance is greater as a thinker and as a designer of decoration and furniture than as an architect, but he did design one building in Lancashire of outstanding importance, and that is **SCARISBRICK HALL,** between Ormskirk and Southport.

There are very few buildings in Lancashire which, if they were excluded from a history of English architecture, would leave a noticeable gap in the story, but Scarisbrick Hall is one of them and would leave a very large hole. Fortunately, when its future was at risk about twenty-five years ago, it was bought by the late Mr Charles Oxley and his wife for use as a school; such it remains, and its future now seems as secure as that of any important building in the County. (It is open to parties by arrangement). One can see it for miles around, as one approaches it across the flat peat-rich fields which were once mossland, or – to be more accurate – one can see the tower and spire which were the last significant parts to be built as the last act in a bitter family feud. Scarisbrick is a house pregnant with the tensions and rivalries which existed between its main builders, Charles Scarisbrick and, later, his elder sister Ann, and between the architects they chose to carry out their commissions, Augustus Pugin followed by his son Edward.

Augustus Pugin was the son of a French émigré draughtsman who had worked in the office of John Nash, the architect of the Brighton Pavilion and the terraces around the Regent's Park in London. He had been trained by his father so well – sketching medieval remains in England and France – that, when his father died in 1832, it was recognised that no-one, not even Rickman, knew more than he did about the details of Gothic art and architecture. He was therefore asked by Charles Barry to help him to produce the decorative details of his entry in the competition for the new Houses of Parliament which, it had been specified, should be 'Gothic or Elizabethan' in their style. This may seem a strange stipulation, since most MPs must have received a classical education and probably lived in Classical houses; but Gothic architecture, being a product of the Middle Ages, was coming to have associations both of antiquity and of the political freedoms linked with the Magna Carta; furthermore, it was thought – wrongly – to have originated in England. When Barry's design won the competition at the end of 1835, his fame was merely confirmed; Pugin's name was made. The previous year he had become a convert to Roman Catholicism, and this strengthened his belief that design in the Gothic style was the only appropriate way in a Christian country.

In 1836 he put this view very forcefully in his book **Contrasts,** when he wrote that 'everything grand, edifying and noble in art is the result of feelings produced by the Catholic religion on the human mind'. It is a view which I do not share, but it won him further fame and also the attention of Catholic patrons like Charles Scarisbrick, who asked him to remodel his ancestral home.

When Augustus Pugin received this commission in 1837, Scarisbrick Hall stood in the form which it had been given between 1812 and 1816 by the Liverpool architect John Slater, who had called in Thomas Rickman, then a scholar rather than an architect, to help him with the necessary 'Gothick' details. Slater and Rickman had not designed a completely new building; rather, they had encased in stone a rambling timber-framed manor house and then added a wing to the west (or left) to give it an air of fitting symmetry. How much more than this is due to Slater and Rickman is not clear from the records, but some of the fittings in some of the rooms behind the Great Hall must date from their time, and there appears to have been a two-storey hall with two tall bay windows, as now, when Pugin began to plan his alterations.

The first room which the visitor sees is the imposing Great Hall to the left of the porch. It is the pièce de résistance of the house and was designed by Pugin to look authentically medieval, as though it was the unchanged heart of the ancestral home of an old-established family. In a way it was, because the Scarisbricks had owned estates in this area since 1238. If one compares it with, say, the hall at Rufford Old Hall, it is at first sight a fairly convincing pastiche, with a screens passage and minstrels' gallery under an ornate oaken roof; it is now the only surviving example of what was a short-lived fashion for

Scarisbrick Hall – Oak Room

'baronial' halls where early Victorian lords of the manor, frightened by memories of the French Revolution and by the upsurge of radical political movements like Chartism, could dispense 'olde Englishe hospitality' to their tenants and guests. At the further (or west) end, high up on the wall, is an immense carving showing Christ crowned with thorns which, traditionally though improbably, was made around 1600 for Antwerp Cathedral. The twisted columns on either side and the accompanying figures of St. Mary and St. John are not part of the original.

This eclectic assembling of separate pieces into a single design is the hallmark of Pugin's work for Charles Scarisbrick, who was a notable collector of antiques. It is nowhere better seen than in the Oak Room (beyond the Great Hall) which serves as an ante-room to Charles Scarisbrick's private quarters in the west wing added by Slater and Rickman. Almost every square inch of the walls is covered by fine Flemish wood carvings which together form a collection which is regarded by scholars as one of the best outside the Low Countries. One has to look closely to decide what is Pugin's work and what is older; for example, the fireplace in the north wall is built with sidepieces designed by Pugin to look like stall ends, while the overmantel is made up with genuine carvings from a sixteenth-century altarpiece like the one at Towneley Hall. The empty niches were originally fitted with statues, but these were sold before the Hall became a school. Since then the large carving in the Hall, all of the panelling in this room and everything else

which I specify in the next three paragraphs have been bought by the County Council, so that they shall stay in the places for which they were designed.

The walls in the Oak Room are dominated by a series of large bas-relief panels, probably carved in seventeenth-century Flanders. The Flood and Noah's Ark on the opposite (west) wall is a scene which everyone will recognise, but many of the others are obscure to anyone whose knowledge of the Old Testament is somewhat shaky. To the left of the Flood is a panel representing the Last Judgement, and several of these panels are in similar pairs, in which a story from the Old Testament is seen as a prefiguration of an event in the New Testament which, in Christian eyes, superseded it – a fairly common procedure for explaining the Bible in medieval times. Thus, on the east wall one can see Moses receiving the Ten Commandments and on the right of that Christ's disciples receiving the Holy Spirit on the first Whit Sunday. Above them and to the left is a panel showing King Solomon and the leaders of the twelve Tribes of Israel placing the Ark of the Covenant in the Temple at Jerusalem; this was regarded as foretelling the New Covenant of the Mass, which is shown in the panel to the left of the fireplace.

The details are fascinating, but I must admit that I find the Oak Room, as a whole, oppressive in its wealth of carving and darkened woodwork. To my mind the most beautiful of the rooms designed by Augustus Pugin is next door – the Kings' Room which,

Scarisbrick Hall – Kings' Room

in its combination of rich but disciplined decoration and superb craftsmanship, foreshadows his masterpiece, the interior of the Houses of Parliament. The room is so called from the series of twenty-seven panels, just below the vaulted cove of the ceiling, which portray most British Kings and Queens from Richard II to Charles I. These were probably painted by Edmund Parris, who was appointed the historical painter to Queen Adelaide (the widow of William IV) in 1838. Most of these portraits were directly copied from those in the Royal collection, and many will be instantly recognisable.

Scarisbrick Hall – Red Drawing Room

The Kings' Room was originally intended as the lobby between Charles Scarisbrick's two libraries in the west wing. What is now the Dining Room on the north was damaged by fire in 1924, but the Red Drawing Room on the south contains a fireplace of great interest, with a pair of paintings on the chimney piece, probably done by Edmund Parris. On the right is a medieval garden where people are singing; to the left is a picture of a man and his wife and their children walking in medieval dress in front of what looks like Scarisbrick Hall. It used to be thought that the man and woman were Charles Scarisbrick and his common-law wife, but it is now believed by scholars that the painting is merely a pretty piece of Romantic nostalgia, the expression of a wish to see the 'present' house in a three or four hundred-year-old setting. Be that as it may, the painting does portray Scarisbrick Hall as Pugin first designed it, and two carved wooden panels towards the top of the spindly main staircase show much the same design. You will recognise immediately the two parallel wings with the hall and its porch between them, but then you will notice that the tower is much lower than the tower which stands today, and that the east wing is considerably less ornate. The records suggest that the house was indeed built as designed by the elder Pugin, but it was certainly changed by his son.

The reason for this is to be found in the death of Charles Scarisbrick in 1860 and in the inheritance of the property by his elder sister, Lady Ann Hunloke. There was no love lost between her and him for several reasons, not least because, when their elder brother Thomas died in 1833, Charles claimed not merely the Scarisbrick estate but also the smaller family estates to which Ann felt entitled. She fought him through the Courts and lost, and he became master of an extensive estate of rich agricultural land, with some coal deposits near Wigan, which brought him an annual income of £40,000. And then there was the question of his 'marriage' with Mary Anne Braithwaite: she had taken his name, borne him two sons and a daughter but, since the marriage had never been solemnised, his children were therefore illegitimate, with all that that involved of scandal among the Catholic gentry of mid-Victorian times. Charles' offence was all the greater in his sister's eyes, since the vast collection of antiques, suits of armour, old books, furniture, prints and paintings by Old

127

Masters was, according to his will, not to descend to her but to be auctioned to provide a trust fund for his children who, as illegitimate, could not inherit the Scarisbrick estates. The sales took about three weeks to complete and raised nearly £45,000. Though Lady Ann came to a virtually empty house in 1861, her rent-roll — for the Scarisbricks by then owned the half of the Manor of North Meols on which the new town of Southport was being built — was about £60,000 per year.

She could afford to build, and she did. On the outside of the east wing one can read an inscription which tells that 'Ann Lady of Scarisbrick built this wing AD 1861 to the memory of her father', but I am not sure how true this is. Maybe I do the woman an injustice, but her house seems less an expression of filial piety than the work of a latter-day Bess of Hardwick: all the work done for her bears her initials 'A.S.', but, to be fair, Charles Scarisbrick's works are also liberally initialled. Edward Pugin, who had worked for Charles Scarisbrick after his father's death in 1852, was asked by Lady Ann to design a new east wing for her and must have felt challenged to rival his father's work. Both client and architect left their mark on the older house.

Edward Pugin was responsible for the painted ceiling in the King's Room which adds so much to its attractiveness; he also designed the knights and coat of arms above the fireplace in the Great Hall; he added modern conveniences like central heating and gas lighting, and a very long service wing to the north. His best work, however, can be seen in the east wing which Lady Ann made her own. Here the Blue Drawing Room is, perhaps, the most beautiful room in the house, with its superb-quality inlaid work in the doors and shutters, its vividly coloured stained glass depicting the Arts and the Sciences and its richly decorated ceiling in which every alternate compartment is painted with the arms of Lady Ann Scarisbrick.

But the exterior of the east wing is the clearest indication of the impact of Lady Ann and her architect, which some would call grossly insensitive to the older work. Edward Pugin gave a greater vertical emphasis to the wing, with tall windows rising into richly gabled dormers which have a very French feel; he added another top to the stair tower and crowned it with fluttering birds which

look like hawks but are meant to be doves (the emblem of the Scarisbricks). Above all, in every sense of the term, he replaced his father's tower, which had been the model for the 'Big Ben' clock tower at the Houses of Parliament, with a taller one with tall windows, pinnacles and a spire to emphasise its height. This he calculated to a nicety, so that it should dominate the ensemble without dwarfing his father's work for Lady Ann's brother. It is thus the supreme example of the tensions of which I wrote earlier, and Lady Ann expressed her thanks in perpetuity by commissioning a stained glass window in the beautiful staircase in the east

Scarisbrick Hall — East Wing

Scarisbrick Hall
– Blue Drawing Room

wing which portrays her and Edward Pugin in adjacent lights. I know of no comparable example. It is just another way in which Scarisbrick is unique.

I have written more words on Scarisbrick than on any other building in the County, but that is a measure of its importance rather than of my liking for it. I am always thrilled, as I approach it down the drive and as the slender tower and then the rambling house unfold themselves to my view; I am always struck by the so carefully calculated contrast between the height and width of the façade, so that neither dominates the other but both co-exist in a creative tension in which each enhances the other; but all this is intellectual fascination rather than emotional affinity. I feel more at ease in Lytham Hall.

I have often sought to analyse this response. It must be due in part to the fact that I cannot regard myself as a Christian in any traditional sense of the term, so that I cannot share Pugin's almost fanatical response to the Middle Ages and his wish to revive its architecture in the totally different circumstances of the nineteenth century. This last phrase gets nearer to the heart of the matter. When Colonel Wilson had himself portrayed in 1773 as a Roman soldier on his daughter's memorial in Lancaster Priory, it was still possible for a gentleman to regard himself as an heir of the Ancient World: society was organised in much the same élitist way; land was a source and symbol of power and was farmed in much the same manner as in Roman times; the classics of Greek and Latin literature were read in contemporary schools and were still the source of myths which had value in explaining contemporary society; and, to get down to harsher realities, warfare was also much the same – at Culloden, the last battle fought on British soil, the disciplined use of cold steel by the Redcoats had destroyed the individualistic élan of the attack by the kilted clansmen under their feudal chieftains.

However, when Hardmans of Birmingham portrayed War in a stained glass window in the Blue Drawing Room, they used in 1862 the symbol of an armoured knight brandishing a sword and a mace – though the rapid-firing Gatling gun had been introduced in the very same year, and the Colt revolver had been in use for a generation. There was too in 1862 a measure of democracy; land was losing its value; the Classics were less read, but children at school did not read medieval works of piety instead; above all, the Industrial Revolution had transformed society from top to bottom. In the 1860s the Middle Ages were more dead than the Graeco-Roman world had been in the 1760s: the Renaissance was just that, a rebirth, a resurrection; the Gothic Revival was fundamentally escapist, a Romantic nostalgia, a form of necrophilia.

129

Augustus Pugin died in 1852, but his ideas on the importance of Gothic architecture inspired many architects for another generation; what is more, such a sentence as 'There should be no features about a building which are not necessary for convenience, construction and propriety' (which he wrote in 1841) was regarded by many in the 1930s as an early justification for 'Modern' architecture. But this is to look too far ahead. In practical terms Pugin's main influence was to encourage the building of churches with details which were not merely approximately Gothic but authentically so, and preferably from the period around 1300, which he regarded as the high point of medieval architectural endeavour. Probably a quarter of the Anglican parish churches in the County were designed something over a hundred years ago with these thoughts in mind; most of them are pleasant enough features in the landscape. The best have attractive spires, as at Wrea Green or Singleton, or pleasing towers like those at Charnock Richard, Whitworth and, especially, Padiham which is an impressively handsome landmark both within and outside the town.

Three churches of this period are, however, outstanding and normally open. All reflect the rivalries between Roman Catholics and Anglicans, once the Emancipation Act of 1829 made it possible for Catholics to build striking churches without breaking the law.

The first in date is in some ways my favourite, **St. Walburge's** in **Preston.** I used to see its spire every day from my office desk. It is a Catholic church built between 1850 and 1854 to the designs of Joseph Hansom, who was also the inventor of the cab. As at Scarisbrick Hall, there is a disproportion between the height of the spire and the breadth of the nave, a contrast which is emphasised by the pure white limestone of the spire and the roughly dressed brown sandstone of the body of the church. As one enters, one is not prepared for the breadth of the church – nearly sixty feet of undivided space covered by a steeply pitched roof borne on spindly hammer beam trusses which carry painted saints under spiky canopies. I find it difficult to like it, but impossible not to be impressed by it. At the east end, the high altar stands well above the nave in a tall large-windowed apse flanked by two other windows at the end of what would normally be aisles. Their tracery is of course copied from models of around 1300. Unfortunately, the fittings at the east end are mostly highly

decorated and assort ill with the bare-boned structure of the church. About the tower (which looks vaguely French) I have fewer reservations, while in combination with the spire it is simply sublime – a three-hundred foot finger of stone pointing heavenwards.

Preston's Anglican **parish church** of **St. John the Divine** is, despite its dedication, less aggressively other worldly and more humane. It is the masterpiece of the little-known Manchester architect, Edwin Shellard, and was completed in 1855. From the outside, with its steeply pitched gables and pinnacled roofs, its well-proportioned spire and its tracery copied from early fourteenth-century

Preston – St. Walburge's Church

sources, it looks like a text-book example of the Decorated parish churches of Lincolnshire, where some of the finest churches of that period were in fact built. This illusion could almost be sustained inside, where the church is divided conventionally into a nave and aisles by arcades of clustered columns with well-carved foliage capitals; however, its hammer beam roofs were not an early fourteenth-century feature.

The church also has some interesting monuments in the chancel, especially an early Georgian one to the wife of Sir Henry Hoghton of Hoghton Tower, and a big Gothic tablet in the south aisle of the chancel in memory of the Reverend Roger Carus Wilson, who encouraged the building of five new churches in Preston before his death in 1839. They are represented in bas-reliefs at the bottom, and one can easily recognise St. Thomas' and St. Mary's.

Preston – St. Walburge's Church

Preston – St. John's Church

131

Perhaps the most beautiful tower and spire in the County belong to what is now **St. Peter's Roman Catholic Cathedral** in **Lancaster** which was designed by Edward Paley, who had been a pupil of Rickman's pupil, Edmund Sharpe. St. Peter's was completed in 1859 to be no more than the parish church for Lancaster's sizeable Catholic community, but has all the grandeur which one associates with a bishop's church. It composes well above the canal and even better if one looks down East Road at the apse, the transept roofs, the roof of the nave, the belfry windows and then the spire itself.

Inside, the church does not have the spatial splendour of St. Walburge's, being designed with the traditional nave and aisles, but the chancel is deeper and vaulted (in wood) and still retains much of its original painted decoration and all of its fine stained glass — as does the west window. The finest decorative feature is, however, the triptych tucked away in the south transept, which used to be the reredos of the high altar. It was designed in 1909 by Giles Gilbert Scott, the architect of Liverpool's Anglican Cathedral, and is beautifully carved and painted with scenes relating to the crucifixion of Christ; it deserves to be seen in a more prominent position.

The stained glass at Lancaster Cathedral, which represents Christ in Majesty in the east windows and the Last Judgement in the great

five-light west window, is fine work by the Birmingham firm of Hardmans. Even better is their richly-hued glass at the Catholic church of **St. Hubert** at **Great Harwood,** which was designed by Edward Pugin in 1858. This includes not merely big set pieces like Christ in Majesty flanked by St. Hubert and St. Mary in the apse, and the story of Adam and Eve in the south chapel, but also little scenes from the lives of the saints which are like the medallions one sees in early medieval windows; it is probably the finest glass of any date in the County.

If one excludes the Nonconformist chapels which I have already mentioned, virtually every mid-nineteenth century church was built in a Gothic style, but once one leaves the field of churches this consensus breaks down. Schools of that date are rare, and most are Gothic. There are two nice examples in Lancaster — Sharpe and Paley's vaguely Elizabethan Royal Grammar School on East Road, which was opened in 1851, and the smaller Girls' Charity School of 1846 on Middle Street which I would attribute to Sharpe. On the other hand, the College of Art on Avenham Lane in Preston was also built in 1846 (as the Institution for the Diffusion of Knowledge) but in a simple Classical style with an ashlar façade above a rusticated basement, with pilasters at the corners and a pedimented portico carried on tall Corinthian columns.

With the possible exception of the frontage building at the White Cross Centre (opposite Lancaster Royal Infirmary) which was built in 1854 as a barracks for the Lancashire Militia somewhat in the style of a Scottish baronial castle, there are only two other Gothic Revival buildings from the middle of the century which are worth going even a short distance to see; both are in Blackburn and appropriately within a stone's throw of the Lewis Textile Museum. The first is now a cinema and gutted of its original features, but it was built as the Cotton Exchange in 1865, with an octagonal two-storey porch leading to a main room well lit with an impressive display of tall bay windows filled with Perpendicular tracery.

The second is the **Blackburn Museum** whose main interest outside is in the panels representing the arts and sciences in medieval dress above the main door and, along the side wall, a fascinating series of bas-reliefs of mid-nineteenth-century trades and industries with, among others, mill-girls and metal workers, a man honing a scythe and a

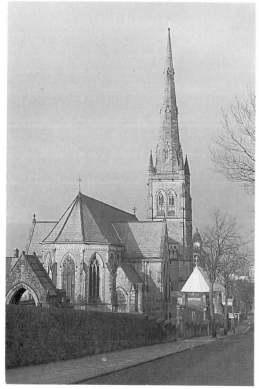

Lancaster — Catholic Cathedral

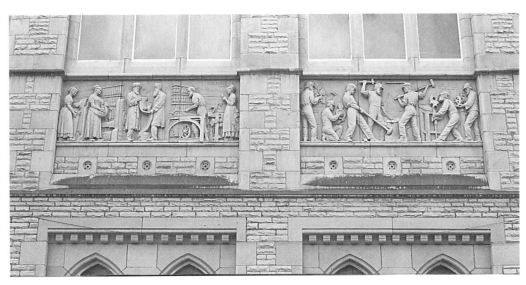

Blackburn Museum

shepherd in a smock. Inside, the customary collections relating to local history and natural history are complemented by a feature of great importance (which ought to be much more widely known). This is the Hart Collection, which contains not merely coins of various dates, but dozens of medieval illuminated manuscripts and even more early printed books; all are works of great interest and some are of considerable beauty.

Standing roughly between the Exchange and the Museum is the original building of the now much-extended Town Hall, which is the earliest of the mid-nineteenth century town halls in the County, finished in 1856 in a richly textured Classical style. With its rusticated ground floor, strongly modelled architraves around the windows, its Corinthian columns and prominent cornice,

it was designed on the model of an Italian Renaissance palace (or palazzo) – a style made popular by Charles Barry. An even more heavily decorated Town Hall is at Burnley, but to my mind it is over-elaborate, and I much prefer the recently restored Mechanics' Institute next door on Manchester Road, which was built in 1854 to the designs of the local architect James Green. In the days before universal public education mechanics' institutes were set up in most Lancashire towns to provide libraries, evening classes and non-religious Sunday Schools. The interior has now been converted to be an arts and entertainment centre, but the fine exterior is just as it was built.

Like the Town Hall at Blackburn, it was designed to look like a palazzo with a rusticated ground floor with plain stonework

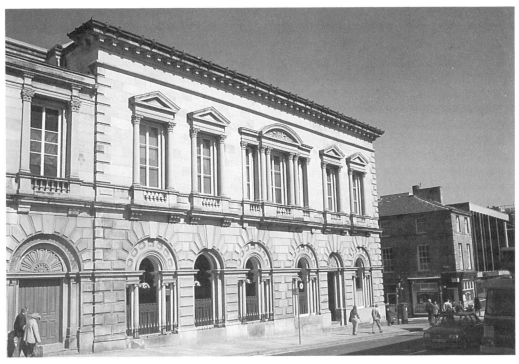

Burnley – Mechanics' Institute

Accrington Town Hall

above. There are six openings on the ground floor of which four have Venetian windows, but only five windows above. This interplay of five openings above six, which places a wide window above the widest pier of the ground floor makes a very sophisticated piece of design; this is certainly the finest Classical façade in Burnley and among the very best of its date in the County.

A more magnificent building, also designed by James Green (who deserves to be better known) was built in **Accrington** between 1857 and 1858. It was called the Peel Institute − in honour of the biggest employers in the town, to whom the former Prime Minister of Corn Law fame was related. It is now the **Town Hall** but originally contained a public hall, as well as the mechanics' institute and news room. This explains the palatial design, with not merely the contrast of rusticated stonework and ashlar, but also a deep carriage porch capped by a pedimented portico carried on no fewer than eight Corinthian columns − clustered in threes at the corners to give a particularly sumptuous effect.

This palazzo style was adopted too for many commercial buildings in the middle of the nineteenth century, and particularly by many banks. The associations between merchants and princes and patrons of the arts like the Medici were too obvious to be overlooked, but taste was changing as well to more richly textured design, as we saw earlier in the Methodist churches at Rawtenstall. Almost every town of any size has at least one fine bank, and there are two palazzi close together on Fishergate in Preston, the Midland Bank and the National Westminster, both designed by J.H. Park in the 1850s. Perhaps the grandest of them all is the National Westminster in Church Street, Lancaster which dates from 1870, but the finest ensemble of mid-nineteenth-century Classical buildings is along **Lancaster Road, Preston,** where J.H. Park designed, on the west side, the Magistrates' Court and Police Station with a forbiddingly massive prison behind. On the east side there is a long line of shops and pubs, built for the Earl of Derby and pulled together into one impressive design by the use of giant pilasters. Later generations were also to add to this street, in their very different but equally impressive ways, the Harris Library, the Co-operative store and, more recently, the new Guild Hall.

By the time that Edward Pugin had finished Scarisbrick Hall in 1868, Gothic was virtually played out as a language of design. Virtually, but not completely, because a number of churches were designed about a hundred years ago as beautiful and as interesting as any others in the County. Most of them were designed by the Lancaster firm of architects, Edward Paley and his partner Hubert Austin, who was the last in what one might call a Lancastrian dynasty of fine architects which went back through Paley and Sharpe to Rickman. Like Edward Pugin, Paley and Austin were not content to design by copying 'authentic' medieval motifs but preferred to create anew, as medieval designers had done, by combining those decorative motifs and structural ideas which pleased them into new and hitherto unknown forms.

Almost every village in North Lancashire has, if not a medieval parish church, one designed by Paley and Austin; almost invariably they are recognisable as such, not because they are copies one of another but because each is well proportioned, pleasingly composed and inventive in its details — and gives the impression of having developed over the years, rather than being the result of a single plan. One of their smallest is St. Mark's at Dolphinholme, with its squat central tower; and St. John's at Galgate is similar. Their biggest church must be St. Silas' on Preston New Road, Blackburn, a dignified building with a fine tower which is a landmark for miles.

More attractive still is the church of **St. John** at **Pilling** which replaced in 1887 the old church which I described in Chapter 5. This has a spire, which is also a prominent landmark, not merely across the now-drained expanse of Pilling Moss — which was once compared to God's grace, because it was infinite — but also across the waters of Morecambe Bay. The spire is recessed behind the tower parapet which, like the chancel, is decorated with tracery-like panels of pink stone inlaid into the rest of the biscuit coloured masonry — what in East Anglian flint and stone would be called flushwork. As is common in Paley and Austin churches, the sides differ: the south of the chancel has a chapel, while the north has a vestry; over all the tower and spire pull the composition together.

Another church which shows well this skill of Paley and Austin in designing buildings which combine well-composed masses with interestingly varied details is at Whittington — an attractive village in the Lune Valley, whose winding main street is lined by several seventeenth-century houses with mullioned windows and highly decorated lintels. It was Paley and Austin too, who were responsible in 1889 for the nave of Hornby parish church — in fact for inserting into the early nineteenth-century 'open-plan' nave the simple arcades and clearstorey which with such distinction and discretion link Lord Mounteagle's tower to his chancel.

Paley and Austin were widely recognised as the best architects of their time in the North West and had a lot of lucrative contracts, including the final remodelling of Hornby Castle which stands proudly above the Wenning Bridge and enjoys fine views up and down the Lune Valley. They were not the only good architects here, and I must mention one more Gothic Revival church which is worth going to see.

St. John's at **Silverdale** was built in 1886 to replace an older church and was designed by the little-known Manchester architects, Ball and Elce. It is faced outside with the local limestone, while the inside walls and the windows, with their flowing tracery, are built of the almost local sandstone which is much easier to carve. In this respect it is rather like

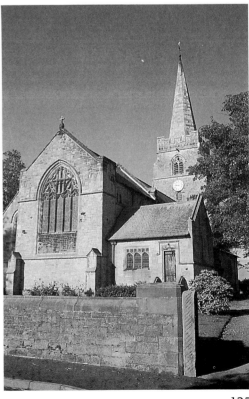

Pilling — St. John's Church

Altcar – St. Michael's Church

Warton Old Rectory which is only a few miles away. All the details are such as one might find in a mid-fourteenth century church. The tower is fine but perhaps too slender, and the interior is pleasant rather than outstanding and somewhat dark. What makes the church more remarkable than most is the quality of the carvings on the capitals of the clustered columns which represent scenes from the Book of Revelation; there is also a stained glass window with an almost photographic portrait of a brother and sister, who look back at one with such intensity that it is hard to believe they have been dead for nearly a century.

As the nineteenth century drew towards its close, it seems in retrospect to have been almost symmetrical in its failed attempt to find a style for itself – not that we in the late twentieth century can look back with any feeling of superiority in that respect, for we are still in James Richards' Age of Confusion. Some form of more or less authentic Gothic dominated the middle decades, but before and after them almost anything was acceptable. The difference was that later nineteenth-century architects were – for want of a better term – more learned than their grandfathers; they knew much more about the details of the past styles from which they drew their inspiration, but they did not strive at all costs to be authentic. For twenty years the variety of styles was once more bewildering, but the quality could on occasion be as high as at any other time.

The most unusual of these late nineteenth-century buildings is **St. Michael's Church** at **Altcar** – between Ormskirk and Formby – which was designed in 1879 by the Chester architect, John Douglas, to replace an older one. If one knows that Douglas designed most of the apparently timber-framed buildings in the centre of Chester, one will not be surprised to find a timber-framed church here – the only one, I think, in Lancashire, though there are three genuinely medieval ones in Cheshire, which are similar to St. Michael's. Inside it resembles nothing so much as a small aisled barn, with square timber posts carrying braces in all four directions – along the nave, across the nave and across the aisles to support the lower parts of the main rafters.

Preston – St. Wilfrid's Church

Preston – Harris Library

The earliest of these late nineteenth-century buildings, **St. Wilfrid's Catholic Church** in **Chapel Street, Preston** is also among the most unexpected. I have perhaps accustomed you to link Roman Catholic churches with Gothic architecture, but here is one which is stridently Classical. It is in fact a remodelling, dated 1874-80, of what old photographs show had been a brick box built in 1793, and therefore hardly distinguishable from a house and detailed inside in the Classical manner. Now everything is far from plain, with a tall plinth faced with rusticated terracotta blocks and surmounted by richly decorated terracotta windows. The interior is even more sumptuous, with ten Corinthian columns of Shap granite to divide the nave from the aisles and carry a richly moulded barrel vault which is penetrated by the clearstorey windows. The apse and the aisles are lined out with Corinthian pilasters between panels of marble, and the apse containing the altar has a coffered half-dome. Everything, no doubt intentionally, gives the impression of a Roman basilica built at the time when the Church Militant had become the Church Triumphant.

A similarly triumphant temple, dedicated this time to Literature, Arts and Sciences, was built a few years later in **Preston** – the **Harris Library and Art Gallery** which rises on a plain, unbroken plinth above the hurly-burly of the Market Place. Traffic has been virtually excluded from the area and a good deal of landscaping work has been carried out in recent years to give 'the Harris' a setting more worthy of its magnificence. It was designed by the local architect, James Hibbert, who was also a Borough Alderman. He travelled widely to seek inspiration for a building which should express the munificence of its founder, the solicitor, Edmund Harris, who left £300,000 for cultural and charitable purposes in Preston. The result was one of the finest buildings in Lancashire, but one which was surprisingly old-fashioned for its time. It was built between 1882 and 1893 but calls to mind immediately Barry's Art Gallery in Manchester or Elmes' St. George's Hall in Liverpool, which were designed in 1824 and 1836 respectively.

Hibbert decided that a version of a Greek temple was the most appropriate model, and various Greek phrases (which I do not understand) are inscribed into the stonework, while the pediment, which is carried on six Greek Ionic columns, contains figures of some of the greatest Greek thinkers and artists. The dedication beneath them is in English, and further inscriptions in English praise the long-lasting value of the mental riches which Prestonians could acquire within these stately walls. A rather overlooked Victorian value was the belief that in a civilised society books and works of art, things which would enrich the mind and broaden one's human sympathies, should be easily available to all without charge.

The façades of 'the Harris' are skilfully designed, but the entrances to each side of the plinth are less than imposing though well worth finding, for the interior is striking with its central rotunda carried on eight Greek Ionic columns, and the collections are interesting too. What one sees, first of all, and most appropriately, on the four sides of the central hall is the vast and very spirited frieze representing the Triumphal Entry of Alexander the Great into Babylon by the great Danish neo-classical sculptor Bertel Thorwaldsen. A much more delicate work in the same room is a cast of Ghiberti's bronze

gate for the Baptistry in Florence which shows scenes from the Old Testament. The first floor rooms contain a rich collection of pottery and glass and a very interesting display on the history of Preston, while the art gallery on the top floor has seven mid-eighteenth-century portraits by the famous Preston artist, Arthur Devis, of which the self-portrait is undoubtedly the most 'alive'.

A very different building — one might say, a less sophisticated building with its array of Flemish Renaissance motifs — is the former Technical School on Blakey Moor, Blackburn, which was begun in 1888; but I like it. I like the combination of red brick and beige terracotta, the bas-reliefs of craftsmen at work, the curling gables and heraldic beasts. Some people regard it as too exuberant, almost vulgar, but its exuberance is controlled — less at the bottom and more at the top and always within a symmetrical framework; it is too easy to get po-faced about architecture and so reduce one's enjoyment of the most public of the arts.

I have only hinted at the variety of styles available to architects in the late nineteenth

Preston — Covered Market

Preston – Miller Arcade

century and only given a glimpse of the wealth of attractive or interesting buildings which lie, half hidden but waiting to be seen by those with eyes to see, in the industrial towns of Lancashire. And some buildings have no 'style' to speak of, being little more than pure structures; but they are none the less interesting for that. I have already mentioned the train sheds at the stations in Preston and Blackburn. In a similar vein is the three-aisled Market Hall at Accrington, which dates from 1868 and stands next to the Town Hall behind an ornate façade. Even more unexpected is **Accrington's Arcade,** a glass-roofed curving tunnel flanked by shops with vaguely Art Nouveau decoration which was built around 1880 to run between Church Street and Warner Street. Even more ornate, with a great display both inside and out of terracotta pilasters and panels of arabesques is the recently restored **Miller Arcade** in **Preston,** built in 1898. But the most striking of these commercial canopies is the larger of **Preston's** two **covered markets,** erected in 1875 just off **Lancaster Road.** Surrounded by a cast-iron colonnade carrying lattice girders, it has a long series of ingenious roof trusses, spanning no less than seventy-five-feet, which create an uncluttered area of nearly an acre.

The king of all Lancashire structures — until recently, at five hundred and eighteen feet, the tallest building in Britain and, with Scarisbrick Hall, the only building which cannot be replicated elsewhere — is, of course, **BLACKPOOL TOWER.** When it was completed in 1894, five years after Eiffel's Tower on which it was admittedly modelled, it made the name and now secures the immortality of the Manchester architects, Maxwell and Tuke; it is also the trademark of this, the greatest of all seaside-resorts. One would have to be a dyed-in-the-wool misanthropist not to enjoy a day-out in Blackpool, for it is probably as true today as it was in 1887 that, as the 'Morning Post' then wrote, it 'offers more fun for less money than anywhere else'. The Golden Mile must be the Prom with the mostest.

Some people lament that one cannot see the Tower's base, that one cannot, as in Paris, stand between four giant feet and look up through the steel lacework to the sky. They have a point but, on the other hand, there is no aquarium, no circus, and no ballroom in the Tour Eiffel. The Tower itself is merely the tallest part of an almost total entertainment complex. The Circus, sitting between the four legs of the tower, and decked out in Moorish finery, can only be visited by those who want to see the show, but the Ballroom is the major architectural attraction of the Tower. It was designed in 1899 by Frank Matcham, the foremost theatre-architect of his day, and is almost overwhelming in the Rococo richness of its decoration. Facing the proscenium arch, which is placed between two big boxes with onion-domes and under statues of the Three Graces, there are two tiers of galleries rippling between the pillars which carry the vaulted ceiling; and this, like every other surface, is encrusted with gilded plasterwork framing pictures of singing and dancing.

For all the exuberant splendour of the Ballroom, the Tower proper is for me the high point of the complex in both senses of the phrase. To take the lift on a fine, clear day and to rise amid a cat's cradle of steelwork, to look at the Fylde spread out as a map at one's feet with a horizon bounded by the mountains of Wales, the Pennines and the Cumbrian Hills, and to see the dwarf structures of the giant gas-rigs in the middle distance and occasionally, the Isle of Man, is an experience never to be forgotten.

Blackpool Tower

Blackpool – Grand Theatre

The Tower Ballroom is not the only building by Matcham in **Blackpool.** He also designed the **Grand Theatre** which was opened in 1894. This was saved in 1972 when the Friends of the Grand Theatre boldy opposed its demolition, skilfully persuaded the owners to repair it for use as a bingo hall and later bought it outright and restored it for use once more as a live theatre in 1981, when it was reopened by the Prince of Wales. We owe them a great debt, for it is the finest theatre in the County. Its façade with its copper-clad dome is ornate but gives no more than a hint of the opulence of the foyer, stairs and bars inside. The auditorium is quite small, but the stalls and three tiers of cantilevered balconies on a horseshoe plan can seat more than 1,200 people in such a way that no-one is more than about sixty feet from the stage. Matcham was a master of his craft and created a theatre whose intimate character is appreciated by actors and audience alike. Everything is richly decorated with gilded and painted plasterwork, with festoons and cherubs. Above all two giant chandeliers hang from the coved ceiling which has six large painted panels portraying (I think) nineteenth-century operatic

composers – wholly appropriate for this most grandiloquent of interiors.

With the Tower Ballroom and the Grand Theatre we have reached the style which, perhaps, more than most typifies the few years on either side of the year 1900. It has been nicknamed Edwardian Baroque, to draw a parallel between it and the grand manner of two hundred years before, which in Lancashire is best exemplified in the hall of Towneley Hall. A building like the **County Sessions House** (now the Crown Court), which stands next to the Harris Library in **Preston,** is even more typical of the style. It was designed in 1899 by the first County Architect, Henry Littler, to replace the sessions house which is now the County and Regimental Museum. The County Council was a mere ten years old but was not going to be outfaced by the Borough's newly-opened Harris Library nor by its tall-spired Town Hall, which faced the Market Place on a site now disfigured by a tower block. So Littler designed a building which should symbolise the County's pride and aspirations, a wide-fronted block, where the vertical emphasis is,

141

Preston – Crown Court

however, just as strong as the horizontal. The centre and two ends are marked by pediments borne aloft by couples of giant Ionic columns rising through two storeys, while above the centre soars a tower which far outtops its then rivals and shows that exuberance of invention in the use of Classical motifs which is the hallmark of the style.

142

The Sessions House was a symbol of the new County Council's ancient pride and modern aspirations; on a smaller scale it was copied in a number of contemporary town halls, of which a pleasing example with heavy keystones to its windows, is at **Great Harwood.** It was designed in 1900 by Briggs and Wolstenholme, who also designed in the same year the Library at Clitheroe whose round tower makes the most of the opportunity provided by a corner site. A slightly similar tower adorns the corner of the bank which stands next to the Town Hall at Great Harwood. In front of them both and forming with them a neat group on the **Market Square,** the best ensemble of small-scale Edwardian design in the County, stands a clocktower; it is square below – with corner pilasters whose stones, like those of the window architraves at the Town Hall, are carved like Gibbs surrounds – and octagonal above, with coupled columns on the narrow faces which do not have clocks. This tower is a memorial to a local cotton manufacturer, John Mercer, who invented a process, called mercerisation, which made it easier to dye cotton cloth.

There is no escaping cotton in Victorian Lancashire, but why should one want to? The slogan 'England's bread hangs by Lancashire's thread' was perhaps an exaggeration, but expressed a profound truth about the economy of Lancashire – as the Cotton Famine during the American Civil War and the collapse of Lancashire's share of world trade after the First World War showed. Every town has buildings donated by its major manufacturers but, strangely enough,

Lancaster, the town which has most, was not so much a cotton-producing town as a town which merely used cotton in its staple products, oil cloth and linoleum. There were two main firms which coexisted by dividing the market between them: the lesser firm, Storey Brothers, concentrated on oil cloth, while the bigger one, James Williamson and Son, employed a quarter of the male population and produced more linoleum than any other company in the world.

Storeys gave the town the vaguely Jacobean-style Storey Institute in 1887 to commemorate Queen Victoria's Golden Jubilee and to house the mechanics' institute as well as a free library and schools of science, technology and art. The younger James Williamson, or Lord Ashton as he had become, presented the town with a park, which contains the Ashton Memorial, and a new Town Hall in the refurbished Dalton Square, both undeniably Baroque. Whereas the Storeys had been content to use Paley and Austin for the original Institute and its extension in 1906, Lord Ashton liked grand gestures and chose famous London architects for his commissions, Sir John Belcher for the Memorial and Edward Mountford for the Town Hall.

Great Harwood – Market Square

The **ASHTON MEMORIAL** in Williamson Park was opened on 23 October 1909 about six weeks before the Town Hall; only two people were waiting to go inside, because nobody knew what this folly of follies was for. As I think Lord Ashton understood it, the Memorial, which a plaque inside the door states is dedicated to the memory of his family – not to his second wife, as the local legends say – was its own justification; it was a perpetually visible reminder, to what he saw as an increasingly ungrateful town, of the benefits which two generations of Williamsons had brought to it. The Park, for example, had been begun during the Cotton Famine to give work to men who would otherwise have been unemployed. Furthermore, by the standards of his time, the second half of Victoria's reign, Lord Ashton was a good employer, autocratic but paternalist. His men earned an average wage (Storeys's men got less) and were not laid off when trade was slack; in the days before National Insurance schemes, men were not retired while they could still do something useful around the factory, and even in retirement received a small pension. In return, he expected loyalty, saw criticism

as opposition and forbade his unskilled staff to join a trade union, preferring to meet deputations of foremen in the study of his house.

With eighty years of hindsight we may say that Lord Ashton had the misfortune of living too long, of being unable to modernise his ideas, his practices, his plant. The breaking point came in the local election of 1911 when in the Skerton Ward, where he and many of his works people lived, the Labour Party candidate came within one vote of victory. Thereafter Lord Ashton (who was a Liberal) declared that he would run the mills 'on economic lines' and take no further interest in the people of his native town. The first threat had little effect; what created greater bitterness was his withdrawal of subscriptions to all Lancaster charities and the winding up of his 'relief committee', for his gifts to Lancaster had amounted to nearly half a million pounds! There can be few people alive now who can remember Lord Ashton; he lived his last years as a virtual recluse and died in 1930. But he still remains an object of dislike in the folk memory of some Lancaster people, and there was

Lancaster – Ashton Memorial

Lancaster Town Hall

opposition to the plans to spend £750,000 on the repair of the Memorial — or 'the Structure', as it is sometimes derisively called.

I for one am glad that the money — much of it coming from outside Lancaster — was spent, for the Memorial is the City's trademark, much more visible than the Castle and Priory. And now it has a use. Standing on the top of a four hundred foot hill, in the middle of the attractive and heavily planted Williamson Park which was laid out in the quarries from which much of the stone to build the town had been extracted, it is of course a belvedere for a view which in many ways is finer than from Blackpool Tower for it includes, as well as the whole of Morecambe Bay backed by the Cumbrian Fells, the Castle and Priory on their hill and the lower Lune Valley. Inside the ground-floor room, which is a delightful venue for chamber concerts and evening functions, there is an interesting exhibition on the life and times and works of the Williamson family; and in the upstairs room there is a spectacular audio-visual show on the gaiety, the drama and the excitements of the Edwardian Age, presented through the eyes of the witty but world-weary butler of a gentry family, like Lord Ashton's.

The Ashton Memorial also contains a model of itself; this is an advantage because,

while it gives little idea of the size of the building (which stands one hundred and twenty feet high at the top of an imposing flight of steps which is nearly fifty feet high) it does enable one to see the details of this, 'the grandest monument in England', at fairly close quarters — which is impossible in a building which stands on a hilltop. Grand it undoubtedly is — with its gleaming white Portland stone and copper-clad dome, its Tuscan porticos on the ground floor and its coupled Corinthian columns around the drum of the dome — but, in my view, it is too elaborate and undisciplined in its details to be really beautiful.

These criticisms do not apply to Mountford's **Lancaster Town Hall** on Dalton Square which was designed a couple of years later when taste was beginning to swing back towards a more restrained flamboyance. The Baroque display is still there in the giant Ionic columns, the heavy keystones to the windows, the play of projection and recession, and the contrast between the shapes of the pediments on the side façades; but the exuberance and the confidence are more tightly controlled and, paradoxically, more effective. The clock tower is heavily modelled, with Tuscan pediments on the cardinal faces, coupled columns on the canted corners and a sinuously outlined dome decked out with round windows and urns, but nothing is done to excess. Even the sumptuous carving of Edward VII and

145

attendant virtues (including Loyalty) is well contained within the widespreading pediment. The Council Chamber, committee rooms and banqueting suite are, unfortunately, closed to the public, but it is possible, with discretion, to enter the foyer and look up the splendid marble-lined staircase to where the portrait of Lord Ashton (who was a small man) looks down on you from on high against a background of his Luneside mills.

The Town Hall was built on the south side of Dalton Square which had been developed speculatively by John Dalton of Thurnham Hall in the years on either side of 1800. Lord Ashton laid out the garden within its balustrade, keeping it level despite the slope, and in the centre commissioned the **Memorial to Queen Victoria.** Her statue in bronze by Herbert Hampton looks in sternly regal splendour across the square towards the Town Hall. Some people are inclined to see in her severe face a silent rebuke to her more pleasure-loving son, but this is no more than the stuff of which the gossip columns are made. There was certainly at the beginning of this century a feeling that a great era had come to end; young people could look forward to a new age of opportunities, but many older people would have looked back with that dread feeling that they would never see Her like again. And so I think that Lord Ashton, who was 59 in 1901, intended his memorial to Queen Victoria to be as well a memorial to the Victorian Age, an idealised portrait of the old Queen herself and, in the

Lancaster – Memorial to Queen Victoria

bronze friezes below her, of other Eminent Victorians – artists, politicians, writers, scientists and public benefactors – who in their various ways had helped to make Britain Great during her reign. Several of them are Lancastrians, like Cobden and Bright, the leaders of the Anti-Corn Law League; the Prime Ministers Lord Derby, Gladstone and Peel; the scientists Edward Frankland, Richard Owen and William Whewell; and, of course, Lord Ashton's father, James Williamson.

Chapter Eight
Our Century's
Contribution

Altham
— Simon Jersey Factory (Harris & Co)

8. OUR CENTURY'S CONTRIBUTION

Lord Ashton – if I am not mistaken – looked back with some nostalgia to the undoubted greatnesses and apparent certainties of the long reign of the Queen Empress. You would be surprised at the number of people I meet some eighty years after her death, who still seem to do the same: they think in particular that the Art of Architecture died with Queen Victoria, and that since then we have lived in a sort of Waste Land. This is a view I cannot share.

I have already mentioned a number of fine or interesting buildings which rose in the early years of this century – the Town Hall and the Ashton Memorial in Lancaster, the Ring Mill at Coppull, the County Sessions House at Preston and the Library at Clitheroe. There are other attractive buildings, too, dating from before the First World War like Kirkham Grammar School or the Girls' Grammar School at Lancaster, and even more from the inter-war period. I also believe that in the forty or so years since the end of the Second World War architects have produced, often against the odds, a number of better-than-average buildings which our children will be pleased to accept as part of their architectural heritage, and that they are designing them as I write these words. I hope that by the end of this chapter, I shall persuade you to agree – if you don't already.

Lord Ashton was not the only philanthropic industrial baron who left his mark on the County of his birth. The first Lord Leverhulme, who was born as William Lever in Bolton, was another. In 1900 he bought the 2,000 acre Rivington estate (which had once belonged to a family called Lever) and between 1902 and 1911 converted 400 acres of meadows near the reservoirs into Lever Park for the benefit of the people of his native town. The Park and estate are now owned by the North West Water Authority. As part of the scheme Lord Leverhulme's architect, Jonathan Simpson, restored and extended – quite sensitively – the two impressive **cruck barns** at **Rivington,** which are sixteenth-century buildings and not Saxon, whatever the local legend says; he also began to build a full-scale replica of the **ruins of Liverpool Castle** as they had been depicted before their demolition in 1720, but it was never completed, and so by the water's edge there is now the ruin of a ruin.

What was perhaps unusual in the Edwardian period was that Lord Leverhulme

Rivington – Hall Barn

created this public park just outside the gates of his own private garden, now known as the **Rivington Terraced Gardens.** These were laid out to the designs of the great landscape architect, Thomas Mawson, who was keen to accept the challenge of creating a garden on what had hitherto been wild and windswept moorland, and vast numbers of trees and shrubs were planted at a considerable cost. Lord Leverhulme's first house, Roynton Cottage, was burnt down in 1913 by a militant suffragette who claimed that Lancashire's wealth was founded on the work of women who were denied the vote. (She may have been right, but Lord Leverhulme was in fact in favour of votes for women). His house was soon rebuilt and later extended, but was demolished after the Second World War, and nothing now remains of it except a few foundations and some floor tiling.

The Gardens survive, however, despite decades of neglect, and have recently been restored to something approaching their original condition by the hard work of members of the British Trust for Conservation Volunteers, as part of a recreation-management scheme for the West Pennine Moors area. They are now very attractive for an afternoon visit and dotted with features like staircases, miniature waterfalls, garden shelters, a seven-arched bridge built of small stones and what is called the Pigeon Tower, a tall, thin summer house

Rivington – Terraced Gardens

which is a landmark on the hillside for miles around. A building for which Lord Leverhulme was not responsible is the low tower a little further up the moor on the top of Rivington Pike; this was built in 1733 as a hunting lodge on the site of one of the beacons lit in 1588 to warn the country of the approach of the Spanish Armada. Consequently, it enjoys superb views.

We are now so used to forty years of peace among the European nations that it is difficult to imagine the scale of the impact of the First World War. There was relatively little hardship on the home front, but such horrendous casualties in Flanders that few families in the land did not lose one of their menfolk. Not surprisingly, therefore, war memorials are among the most important structures of the 1920s, and a number were placed on the Statutory Lists of buildings of special architectural or historic interest during the recent resurvey for the Department of the Environment. Most of them, like those at Accrington or at Preston, rely for their effect on symbolic figures of Compassion or Victory standing against obelisks with Classical details. More realistic is the memorial at **Oswaldtwistle** where a bronze soldier with fixed bayonet stands over a wounded comrade to protect him; more moving, perhaps, as a symbol of the sheer enormity of the sacrifice, is the immense granite obelisk at **Blackpool** which, with bronze bas-reliefs of service men and women at its foot, stands between two tomb chests bearing the names of the dead.

To me the most poignant of all the testimonies of the Great War is, however, in one small room at Astley Hall: the contrast between the photographs of young men kitted up in a drill hall before they left, as the 'Chorley Pals', to form part of the East Lancashire Regiment and the hundreds of names in the Book of Remembrance. . . To the best of my knowledge, the only parish in Lancashire which received back all the young men who had left it for King and Country was Arkholme in the Lune Valley.

When advising its inspectors about what sort of inter-war buildings to add to the Statutory List, the Historic Buildings and Monuments Commission (HBMC) proposed three headings of style – Classical, Modern and 'Others', the catch-all phrase which embraces all oddities. I cannot think of a better way to organise the variety of fine buildings which we have inherited from the 1920s and 1930s, so I shall use it in the pages which follow.

Classical architecture had a last fling in the inter-war period; or perhaps I should say its penultimate fling, because a small number of buildings based on Classical motifs have begun to re-appear in recent years. Forgetting the present for a while – except to say that I have the same mental reservations about a Classical Revival in the 1980s as I expressed about the Gothic Revival in the 1860s – a number of memorable buildings in the Classical tradition were built about half a century ago, and I have little doubt that some of them will in time be listed and thereby accorded the measure of protection which they deserve.

The earliest of these is the **Convalescent Home** built between 1925 and 1927 on the North Shore at **Blackpool** for the miners of Lancashire and North Staffordshire. It is a monumental three-storey design by the Bolton architects, Bradshaw, Gass and Hope, in the restrained grand manner of the late seventeenth century with red bricks and ample stone dressings, set back so that it can be easily appreciated. In its scale it is symbolic both of the importance of coal mining to Lancashire and of the dangers which miners incurred. It covers a lot of ground, but the inevitable horizontal emphasis is countered by a central tower, narrow projecting wings, stair turrets and tall chimneys, which stress the building's height.

Burnley, on the other side of the County, has, for reasons which I cannot explain, perhaps the best collection of inter-war Classical buildings – starting with what was the head office of the **Burnley Building**

Blackpool – Miners' Convalescent Home

Society on Grimshaw Street. It was designed by Briggs and Thorneley of Leeds and stands next to a florid Florentine palazzo, built as the Manchester and County Bank in 1876. The Building Society office, which is now occupied by the Borough Council, was completed in 1930 and shows very clearly the evolution in taste over fifty years towards much simpler designs. Only the central features on the entrance front and side façade are emphasised with giant columns with approximately Corinthian capitals; the rest of the building is composed of relatively plain expanses of walling.

Next door on the other side stands the **Borough Library,** a building with a somewhat French feel to it, which was designed by George Hartley, the Deputy Borough Surveyor, and again completed in 1930. Here too the contrast between the plainness of the apparently single-storey sides and the ornately monumental character of the two-storey projecting centrepiece, which fronts the top-lit Library hall, is very marked. The actual entrance is deeply inset between two giant Corinthian columns up an imposing flight of steps, doubtless to give the impression, as at the Harris Library in Preston, that one is entering a temple of the arts.

Opposite these two inter-war buildings is the **Magistrates' Court and Police Station** which was not completed until 1953, to the designs of Bradshaw, Gass and Hope. Since in its restrained 'neo-Georgian' style it is comparable to the Municipal Offices which they had built in Bolton just before the War, I used to think that its construction was delayed by the outbreak of hostilities. However, I understand that the plans are dated 1950, so this building with its four column Ionic portico to emphasise the centre must be the last example in Lancashire of the Classical tradition, half a generation 'out of date' at the time of its completion.

Another of Bradshaw, Gass and Hope's Classical designs which was in fact completed shortly before the War – in 1938 – is the **Town Hall and Library** at **Padiham.** This is a real period-piece which still retains all its original fittings, including the electric fire in the former Town Clerk's office! Outside it is faced in brickwork with a slightly projecting Corinthian portico of stone, above which is a little cupola-cum-clock turret which looks more Scandinavian than English.

The most monumental Classical ensemble in the County of any date is the **Edge Hill**
152

College of Education. This was built on a hill to the south-east of **Ormskirk** to the designs of the County Architect, Stephen Wilkinson. It has been greatly extended to the rear, but the attractive brick and stone façades which face St. Helens Road are just as they were built in 1931, with strongly projecting wings and a two-storey centre block, emphasised by paired Corinthian columns and a copper-covered square turret.

Later in the 1930s Wilkinson's office produced a number of public buildings in a more 'stripped-down' Classical style, as a somewhat belated response to the (I believe, justified) assertions of Le Corbusier , Mies van der Rohe and other proponents of the self-styled 'Modern Movement' that architectural beauty results more from good proportions than from Classical details. The best examples of this trend in Lancashire are at **Accrington,** where the **Magistrates' Court** and its neighbouring **Fire Station** on Manchester Road were built in 1933 to the designs of Percy Thomas. The Classical details in the Magistrates' Court are reduced to a pediment over the entrance door (which is set in a monumental block looking

Padiham Town Hall

somewhat like a triumphal arch), while the hose-drying tower at the Fire Station has another pediment, and the garage doors are framed by a sort of squared-off colonnade. There are similar Classical allusions rather than Classical details at the Kingsway Centre in Lancaster, where the entrance is set behind a sort of portico with two pilasters and two columns which are fluted but have no capitals. The building, designed by Frederick Hall, the Borough Engineer and Surveyor, was completed just before the War began, and with it — but for the Burnley Magistrates' Court — the Classical tradition died.

In reality, of course, life is not as neat as that, and while the Classical tradition was in terminal decline, the Modern Movement was beginning to influence architectural design in England. As always, it was the decorative, rather than the structural, aspects which first found favour. I have already hinted at this by writing of a 'stripped-down' Classicism, the gradual reduction in the use of Classical motifs and increasing reliance for architectural effect on good proportions and the interplay of larger and smaller masses and of plain and decorated surfaces. An early and attractive example of this is the **Library and Lecture Hall** in the centre of **Thornton** which was designed in 1937 in Stephen Wilkinson's office. A more showy example is what is now the **Prestige factory** on Colne Road, **Burnley.** This has considerable historic interest because, in 1937, it was probably the first ever factory built at the expense of a local

authority to encourage new industries to develop in a town whose staple industry — in this case cotton weaving — was in decline. With its simple rectangular masses, its sheer brickwork above big windows and its columns at the entrance which carry, not Classical capitals, but flaming torches, it was designed by the London architects, Wallis Gilbert and Partners, to suggest that factories could be exciting and interesting places rather than dark satanic mills.

There are only three buildings in Lancashire which the leaders of the Modern Movement would have been content to acknowledge, and two of these are at seaside resorts — perhaps because clients are inclined to be more adventurous at places associated with holidays rather than with the routines of work. The earlier of the two is the **Midland Hotel** built by the London, Midland and Scottish Railway in 1933 on the seaside opposite the station at **Morecambe.** It is a three-storey white-painted building designed by Oliver Hill on a gently curving plan, concave on the entrance side where the tall window of the staircase tower offsets the long sweep of the projecting stringcourses above the windows. On the seaward side, the main reception rooms enjoy the wide views over the Bay which makes Morecambe the most attractive, if not the most exciting, of Lancashire's seaside resorts. Inside the hotel the most engaging features are three bas-reliefs by the famous sculptor Eric Gill - one in the ceiling of the staircase tower showing

Morecambe — Midland Hotel

Blackpool – Casino

the sea-god Triton and some mermaids, and two others in the room at the end of the left-hand corridor called, appropriately, the Eric Gill Suite. The first, which is a pictorial map of Morecambe Bay, has always been in its present position but it has recently been joined by a large panel of polished Portland stone carved in low relief to represent a scene from Homer's **Odyssey**, symbolising hospitality, where the princess Nausicaa welcomes the shipwrecked Odysseus to her island home with the words, 'There is good hope that thou mayest see thy friends'.

The second Modern building is the circular **Casino** at the **Blackpool Pleasure Beach** which was completed just before the War in 1939, as part of a plan to bring the Pleasure Beach up to date. It was designed by Joseph Emberton to accommodate restaurants and a flat for the owner, but has been completely altered inside, although the essential structure of reinforced concrete with ribs radiating from a central core to support the floors is unchanged. So too is the outside appearance with its sweeping circular balconies, its corkscrew staircase and thin spiral tower by the doorway which looks like

a miniature helter-skelter — quite appropriately at the entrance to what claims to be Europe's greatest amusement park.

The third of these Modern buildings is the **Co-operative store** just beyond the covered market on **Lancaster Road, Preston.** It may not look very controversial now, half a century later, but, when it was built in 1937 to the designs of W.A. Johnson of the CWS, it was something of a landmark, since it showed unmistakably that it was a steel-framed building. If you compare it with the nearby Town Hall, which was built four years previously, you will see what I mean. The Town Hall, too, has a steel frame, but it is clad with a thin layer of Longridge stone; one can guess that the stone walls are no more than a skin from the fact that the glass in the windows is almost flush with the surface of the walls. In the Co-op, however the steel structure is clearly expressed and is used as the basis for such decoration as the façades display, since the first and second floor windows are set back behind the structural steelwork. Such structural 'honesty' was one of the virtues which the Modern Movement claimed for itself.

The HBMC's third category for inter-war buildings – Others – only includes in my view two buildings of interest, the extension to **Blackburn Cathedral** and the relocated Claughton Hall.

After the creation of the Anglican Diocese of Blackburn in 1926, it was felt necessary to expand the old parish church to make it a more worthy setting for a bishop's throne and the accompanying ceremonial. So the old very shallow chancel was taken down, and a new one preceded by north and south transepts in a simple Gothic style with rockfaced stonework was begun to the designs of W.A. Forsythe. Everything stands on a massive basement, built on the steeply sloping site to accommodate vestries, meeting rooms and a library. The War intervened, however, before the work could be finished; funds which had been adequate in 1939 were no longer so in 1961, and W.A. Forsythe had died. The decision was therefore taken to appoint Laurence King to complete the work on a less sumptuous scale; instead of the massive central tower originally planned, a glazed octagon of reinforced concrete was raised above the crossing, and it casts a golden glow over the high altar and the

spiky metal-work crown which hangs above it. Externally this octagon is perhaps even more effective, since it composes well with the original western tower; the lantern is lower and wider than the tower, but the slender spire above it rises even higher as the principal focus of the design.

The most striking of all the inter-war buildings in Lancashire is not open to the public and does not really date from the 1930s at all, except that the older pieces from which it was assembled were put together – Lego-like – between 1932 and 1935. **Claughton Hall** used to stand down by the old church in the Lune Valley village and had done so since the seventeenth century when it was built for the Croft family. A wing still stands by the church, but the bulk of the house was moved half a mile and 300 feet up the hill and reassembled by the architect Harry Fairhurst, more or less as originally built, but with the addition of an upper hall based on crucks from a barn in Herefordshire. Fairhurst was working for Edmund Morse, the Managing Director of Williamson's, the company of the late Lord Ashton. Was it meant to be symbolic that the twin-towered country house of a new industrialist could

Blackburn Cathedral

now outstare the modernised pele tower of Hornby Castle? Such an act — some would say, of vandalism — could not be undertaken today, because the listed building legislation would prevent it. By and large, I suppose I am glad, but an age which does not permit follies runs the risk of hobbling human creativity.

The Second World War interrupted the history of building in this country much more than did the First. For a start, it was half as long again, and for nearly six years the creative work of British architects and engineers was directed at self-defence and the destruction of the loathsome Nazi Empire. The material damage sustained was far greater too, and at least another six years were to pass before the war-time controls on building were more or less relaxed, and thought could be given once more to new building rather than to reconstruction. Furthermore, Britain was a much poorer country in 1945 than in 1918, and the necessary resources were more difficult to find: with a few obvious exceptions, like the Royal Festival Hall in London which set out to prove in 1951 the untruth that Britain was back to pre-war normality, the watchword in building was quantity not quality.

It is difficult for us who have grown up in the post-war years — and we must be at least two-thirds of the present population — to appreciate the buildings which have been put up during our life-time. We are not predisposed to like contemporary architecture because of its semi-nostalgic associations with the 'good old days'; it is almost always devoid of allusions to past styles and has to be judged by purely aesthetic criteria — about which we are not taught in school; there is so much of it around us, and so much is no more than mediocre, that, unless we are professionally involved in it, we tend to close our eyes to it all and assume that it is all unworthy of our attention, unless like Centre Point it is associated with controversy, or like Ronan Point with disaster.

Anyone who talks or writes about present-day buildings therefore invites debate and, sometimes, passionate disagreement. I am content to run this risk because, while I believe that it is more difficult to produce good buildings in the intellectual and economic climate of the later twentieth century, I also believe that, despite this, some contemporary developers and their architects are producing buildings of which we can be proud, which the Department of the Environment will list in due course, and which our children will be pleased to inherit and protect as part of their heritage. The last pages of this chapter will describe some of them.

Buildings are always a reflection of the society in which they are produced. One of the factors which militate against the production of good buildings in the later twentieth century is the lack of an identifiable user for most intended buildings. The majority of offices, shopping developments, factories and houses are built speculatively and are therefore designed for cheap construction and average requirements, rather than to meet the specific needs of a known person — as was normal until the beginning of this century. In these circumstances it is difficult for an architect to produce more than an average design. When, however, a modern building **is** designed for an identified client with known needs, which transcend short-term commercial considerations, it is almost always higher than average in its quality and interest.

One of the largest post-war developments in Lancashire and certainly the most successful **town-centre** development in the County — and, probably, one of the best in Britain since its first phase won a Civic Trust Award in 1969 — is at **Blackburn.** It was begun in the mid 1960s and carried out by the Laing Company for the Borough Council with Mary Smallbone of the Preston firm of Building Design Partnership (BDP) as project architect. Its success — and I mean its success in terms of urban design, although its commercial success seems convincing as well — is largely due to its scale; it is seen as a town-centre development, rather than a suburban one transplanted to a town centre, because it is fairly tightly knit and the buildings are generally three or four storeys high, with car parks on the upper levels. On the other hand the public footways are generously wide and, when covered over, are not too low, and there are also welcome

Claughton Hall

Blackburn Town Centre

Blackpool – Hounds Hill

breaks where one can sit out in the sunshine with trees and flowers and, in one case, a pool: in most places it is pleasant to be there. The massing of the buildings is bold, the number of materials used is small, and the details are generally robust enough to withstand the inevitable attempts at vandalism. Above all, though there are shops on upper levels, it is possible to walk through the whole development at ground level, and it has recently been integrated with pedestrianised streets to the west.

One of the most pleasing features of this new town centre is the way in which it is advertised from afar by the presence of a tower block (clad in brown tiles like so much of the development) which is not just another rent-producing slab, as Sir John Betjeman called them, but the vertical extension of the Town Hall. When one compares Blackburn's town centre with Preston's, where the once attractive skyline has been scarred for the lifetime of anyone reading this book by the intrusion of ill-proportioned office blocks and flats, it is clear how wise Blackburn Borough Council was when it continued the traditional practice, whereby the only buildings which were allowed to rise above the average height were buildings of significance to the community as a whole, like churches or public buildings.

It would be unwise for me – and boring for you – to name all the town-centres in Lancashire which have been disfigured by office blocks or demeaned by shopping-precincts which are too small in scale for their surroundings; my purpose in writing this book is to be positive, to emphasise excellence. I am, however, sad that there is, in my view, only one other town-centre shopping development which can stand comparison with the one in Blackburn. It was designed by Keith Scott and Terry Devlin of BDP and stands in **Blackpool** at **Hounds Hill,** within a hundred yards of the Tower. As at Blackburn, the car park is above the shopping-malls, so that they can be walked through at ground level.

Inside, the development is much the same as anywhere else with the normal mix of multiples on either side of the walks; what is, however, impressive is the way the exterior

157

Lancaster — Mitre House

of the precinct has been integrated into much of the rest of the town centre, with richly moulded hard red brickwork, cast-iron and glass canopies, and an attractive carved brick bas-relief of frolicking holiday-makers by the seaside, which is placed over the principal entrance. It well deserves the Civic Trust Award which it won in 1982.

There may be others, but I can only think of one speculative office development in Lancashire which reaches anything like an acceptable standard in terms of urban design as well as internal convenience, and that is **Mitre House** in **Lancaster**. And that success was largely due to the skill of the consultant architect William Whitfield who, at the insistence of the County Planning Department — a story which is too long to tell here — was invited by the original architects to suggest ways of reducing the impact of an enormous office block on the very visible hillside site below the Priory and the Castle. It was he who suggested that the proposed monolithic slab should be broken up into a number of smaller blocks set at right angles to one another in such a way that they should read as a series of buildings, in which none would dominate the others, and some roofs should be in the shadow while others reflected the sun. The result is not, perhaps, great architecture but is a brilliant piece of urban design, which breaks up the scale of the building so that the City's two most historic monuments are not outfaced; it won a well-merited Civic Trust Award in 1978.

I do not think that many speculatively built office blocks will be regarded as part of the County's heritage in a generation's time, but

I believe that a number of buildings built for their own use by local firms will be appreciated then, perhaps more than they are now, as their qualities become more evident. Two such buildings of the 1960s are Sagar House, at the southern end of the village of Eccleston near Chorley, and a shop in New Street, Lancaster.

Sagar House at **Eccleston** was designed by William Field and built in 1966 as a two-storey office block for the textile firm of Carrington (which, however, recently stopped production in the village). In its utmost simplicity it is a text-book example of Modern Movement design — a well-proportioned steel-framed box faced with sheets of glass carried by thin fins of steel which provide the only vertical emphasis. This sheer effect is offset by a projecting canopy at the entrance and by a windowless wall faced with slate which projects at right angles on the right, but these contrasting elements serve only to underline the exquisite refinement of the main block itself.

Kenneth Gardner's **shop** in **New Street, Lancaster,** was originally built as a branch of Martin's Bank shortly before it was amalgamated in the late 1960s with the neighbouring Barclay's Bank. It is obviously of its date but fits in well with its neighbours of about 1880 and 1750 because it respects their scale and their proportion. I do not know what the original ground-floor arrangement was — it is now a wide shop window. The building is about three times as wide as the average Georgian building in New Street, and therefore the architects, Green, Lloyd and Adams, took pains to reduce its

Lancaster – Shop in New Street

accommodate the Chief Executive's Department. It relates well to the scale of the older building and follows the short-lived fashion set by the architects Yorke, Rosenberg and Mardall for buildings in which the glazed outer skin is set behind the structural framework of the building. A conscious decision was taken that all the finishes in the building should be of high quality so that, although more expensive at first, they would need little maintenance later; the wisdom of this decision has been more clearly shown with every year that passes.

apparent width by giving it a steeply-pitched hipped roof and by emphasising the vertical elements of the windows; they also disguised the extra height of these windows by placing a sort of balcony in front of each of them, so that what one sees is a window of roughly the same proportions as those in the neighbouring houses but set in a taller frame. If only all contemporary buildings in old townscapes were designed with such care!

From the 1970s we have an equally successful design, produced in the office of the County Architect, Roger Booth, for what is called the **Christ Church Precinct** of the County Hall at **Preston.** The old 'Norman' façade of John Latham's Christ Church was kept, and behind it a large three-storey complex was built above a car park to

A somewhat similar **office building,** which won a Civic Trust commendation for the Kevin Fletcher Smith Partnership in 1978, is set back on the east side of **Station Road** in **Bamber Bridge.** It is now occupied by a firm called B & R Taylor but was built as the regional office for a firm of timber suppliers; the standard of the internal wooden fittings (which are not visible to the public) is therefore very high. Externally, it is just as pleasing, with its glazing set back behind the structural framework, which is faced in dark red brick, and with the beams which carry the flat roof projecting forward to provide a slight canopy to the upper windows.

Another successful **municipal office,** though more unassuming than the Christ Church Precinct, is at **Clitheroe,** where it was designed by staff architects under the Borough Architect, Charles Wilson, to house most departments of the Ribble Valley Borough Council. It is built across the slope of the land, which allows a measure of car

Bamber Bridge – Office Building

Lancaster – Bath Mill Estate

parking and service accommodation to be tucked in under the building. In keeping with the small market town in which it stands, it is in no way grandiose, but composed of small-scale blocks never more than three storeys high, and its entrance, normally approached from the town centre under an archway opposite the Library, is sturdy and welcoming. Its long lines of windows and generally sparse detailing make it an obviously modern building, but its pitched roofs and limestone walling give it a traditional feel and won it a Civic Trust commendation in 1982.

In the matter of contemporary housing I have little doubt that the majority of developments which will be highly regarded in a generation's time will have been produced in the public sector where, despite the difficulties of working down to government-inspired Housing Cost Yardsticks, more thought was given to adequate standards of accommodation within houses and to the provision and layout of the space between houses than was normally the case in private estates. One of the finest examples of this is on the **Bath Mill** site in **Lancaster.** It stands above the canal, with superb views over to the Castle and Priory on their hill, and across Morecambe Bay to the Lake District. The terraces of houses are built of rendered blockwork with traditional pitched roofs and window surrounds and have been given individual front gardens, grouped around flagged courtyards from which cars are banished; their backyards are separated from the

footways by walls of the local sandstone, in order to integrate the development better with the traditional neighbourhood of stone-built houses. The success of the estate, which was designed by John Angell of BDP for the North British Housing Association, and its popularity with its tenants, are reflected in the fact that it is (I think) the only contemporary housing estate in the country to have been designated as a Conservation Area. This measure was thought to be necessary to prevent the disfigurements which nearly always occur when tenants exercise their right to buy and seek to 'personalise' their houses – to the detriment of a carefully designed streetscape. The estate also won a Civic Trust Award in 1980.

Something of the same care to recreate the better features of traditional housing in terms of contemporary design can be seen in houses recently built by Preston Borough Council as part of the rehabilitation of the Plungington area which was first developed about 120 years ago. These red brick houses, traditionally detailed with stone dressings and set in small private gardens with generous public open space around them, came close to a commendation by the Civic Trust a few years ago.

Among the best housing developments which the private sector has to offer is **Astley Village** near Chorley, where a number of developers were given permission to build small estates according to design briefs drawn up by the Central Lancashire New Town Development Corporation. The individual houses are fairly standard in their design, but

One of the most striking modern buildings, designed using bold constructional techniques to be a landmark and therefore to remind one of its existence even though it may not be beautiful, is the **restaurant** at **Forton Service Station** on the M6. Like the new water tower on Scarth Hill near Ormskirk, it always reminds me of a concrete mushroom. It is hexagonal in plan and supported on six reinforced-concrete ribs, which form the frame of the forty-foot stalk on which it stands. It was designed by T.P. Bennett. The roof-top viewing platform is no longer open to the public, but from the transport café on the upper floor there is a very fine view, which extends on a clear day from Blackpool Tower to the Bowland Fells and from the Cambrian mountains to those of Cumbria.

A mile or so to the south of the Forton service station is probably the most attractive **motorway bridge** in Lancashire; it was designed in the office of the County Surveyor, James Drake, to carry a minor road over the M6 by **Scorton** church – a pretty little building by Paley and Austin with a red tiled roof and a spire covered with wooden shingles. There is a similar bridge over the Clitheroe bypass, but the Scorton one looks better because of its setting, especially when seen from the south, since one looks down to it and it composes well with the church. What pleases me most about it is the controlled asymmetry of its cantilevered spans as it sweeps down the hillside with the longer span leaping over the twin carriageway of the M6, while the shorter one anchors it into the hillside.

Forton – Service Station Restaurant

are laid out with care around culs-de-sac or on a network of footways (with separate road access) all set within dense planting of trees and shrubs. This gives a greater degree of privacy than is common on speculatively built estates. Now that private developers have been encouraged by town planners to produce housing estates of higher quality, the expectations of the public have been raised, and it will probably be difficult, unless the economy takes a significant downward turn, for standards to be lowered again.

Scorton – Motorway Bridge

Most industrial buildings are now built speculatively on industrial estates, as local authorities vie with each other to attract businesses and thereby employment to their areas. Most of them offer simple but adequate accommodation and services under a single-storey shed which is no more than competently designed. It is, therefore, all the more welcome to find a building which by virtue of neat detailing or better than average proportions stands out from the crowd. One such set of buildings was designed in 1985 by the Leeds architects, Fletcher, Ross and Hickling for the **NORI Brickworks** near **Accrington** at the east end of Whinney Hill, whose flanks have been quarried for a hundred years to provide building stone and brick earth. If it were not for the giant letters NORI painted outside, one might not know what went on in these vast sheds, though the well-detailed brickwork in some of the end walls, and the hard landscaping (again made of red bricks) which contrasts well with the shining steel roofs with their attractive curved eaves, would probably give the game away.

Perhaps the finest, and certainly the most striking, of all the recent industrial buildings in Lancashire stands a couple of miles away in the **Altham** Enterprise Zone. It was designed in 1987 by Philip Bintliff of Studio BAAD to house the **offices and garment store of Simon Jersey the Uniform Company.** Three-quarters of the total area of the building is devoted to the garment store which is clad with profiled steel sheeting, set inside the structural framework so that the internal wall surfaces are smooth and uninterrupted. The reverse is true of the two-storey office section; as befits a company which is involved in clothing design, this is faced with large panels of reflective double glazing which gives a very stylish external finish and a pleasingly well lit interior to the open-plan offices. All in all, this is a building which justifies my belief that buildings are better designed, when designed for users whose requirements are known to the architect.

Churches and schools have long tended to be designed to a well-defined brief and therefore to be among the most interesting buildings of any age, and the same is perhaps even more true today. Almost all the County schools of the last twenty or thirty years, and especially primary schools, are worth more than a second look, but to my mind the finest educational buildings are to be found in **Lancaster.**

Lancaster – St. Martin's College Library

Among the best is the **Library of St. Martin's College of Education,** a building of the late sixties designed by Charles Pyke and Partners, with totally glazed walls set within the reinforced concrete structure of the building. This is more interesting than most in its form since, at the ground floor level, it has single pillars which get wider as they grow taller and, at the level where they carry the beams of the first floor, split into two narrow 'prongs', rather like a tuning fork, only to join again at the top where they support the roof. It is difficult to see this inventiveness of structural form being countenanced in a speculative development, but the variety of shape and texture and shadow which it creates adds greatly to the pleasure one can derive from the building. In its general lightness, this contrasts strikingly with the solid masonry of the nearby perimeter wall and castle keep, which were originally built in 1880 as part of a barracks for the King's Own Royal Regiment.

The finest of all the recent educational ensembles in the County is, without a doubt, **Lancaster University,** which received its Royal Charter in 1964. It is virtually a small hill-town, built about three miles south of Lancaster around a spinal avenue on an often windswept ridge called Bailrigg which enjoys superb views over the Fylde and Morecambe Bay. From a distance it always reminds me of a luxury liner stranded on the hillside, because the lower parts of almost all the buildings – which must stretch nearly half a mile from north to south – are faced with pale yellow brickwork, while the very varied shapes of the 'superstructure', except for the great tower, are painted white.

As one approaches it across its parkland setting, and up the road which is beautifully engineered into the landscape, the brilliance of its urban design, by the architects Shepheard and Epstein, becomes more apparent. All the car-parks are on the perimeter, so that the centre is one long pedestrian precinct, centred on Alexandra Square — named after Princess Alexandra who is the University's very popular Chancellor. The Square is aligned east and west, so that part of it can be always in the sunlight; the Spine runs north and south and is protected from the prevailing winds by ranges of buildings on the west — though it is also open to the sunshine because it is only half covered. It is not just a long corridor, because it broadens into gardens at intervals on the eastern side. All the teaching and residential accommodation is built around courtyards, so that the place always feels complete, like a contemporary Oxbridge College; this was doubtless a factor in winning it a Civic Trust Award as early as 1968. None of the architecture is really great, though the Great Hall is rather fine, and the **Chaplaincy Centre,** which I shall mention again later, is both interesting and quite moving. Great architecture is, however, a luxury which one can forego, when the general standard of one's surroundings is so pleasingly high.

I must have written nearly as many words in this book about churches as about houses, but that is hardly surprising; whatever our detailed standpoints, most of us would agree that a man's relations with himself, his neighbours and the natural world — to express it no more theologically — are matters of considerable importance to his well-being, and that in a society, which is still nominally Christian, those concerns are focussed in churches. And so it is that I shall bring this chapter to a close by describing a few places of worship.

But what should a church look like? The days are long since past when a vague allusion to the Gothic style would automatically identify a religious building; in default of any other sign it is now a cross which, appropriately, designates a church. This is certainly true of the Anglican **Church of All Saints, New Longton** (designed in 1963 by Tom Mellor and Partners) which might otherwise be mistaken for, say, a library. It is a plain square room with a pyramidal roof and is lit by windows in the west wall and at the top of the other walls, so that all the congregation's attention is focussed on the altar, which is lit from above, or on the pulpit which stands close to it.

A much more traditional church is the Roman Catholic **Shrine of Our Lady of Lourdes,** near the Victoria Hospital in **Blackpool,** which was built as late as 1955 to the designs of the Liverpool architect, Francis-Xavier Velarde. The interior of the church is very simple and restrained, with glazed screens placed high in the walls to concentrate attention on the altar, and unmoulded semi-circular arches to every opening; only the gold mosaic on the round pillars of the arcades adds a touch of splendour. Outside, the Portland stone building is capped by a copper roof and a

Lancaster University
— Alexandra Square

partly gilded spire which is the first thing one notices as one approaches, but above the west door is a bas-relief of Christ on the Cross with God the Father above his head and the dove of the Holy Spirit at his feet – very medieval in design if not in execution.

A much more assertively modern church, with a skeletal bell tower and a spreading canopy over the west door is **St. Mary's Roman Catholic Church** in **Leyland** which was designed in 1959 by Weightman and Bullen. It too is unconventional in form, since it is round, with a crinkly copper-covered roof capped with a central lantern which funnels light onto the high altar. This altar is placed in the centre of the church, and around the circular 'nave', outside the Y-shaped pillars which support the roof, is a series of chapels lit with attractive panels of stained glass.

Leyland – St. Mary's Catholic Church
Preston – Mosque

Variety of belief and practice has long been a hallmark of religious life in Lancashire, and the post-war world has seen the arrival of Islamic communities to add their perceptions and understandings to those of a community which, hitherto, has basically been Christian. Until recently most Islamic congregations have worshipped in converted premises, but in 1987 a purpose-built **mosque** was completed to the design of Thomas Hargreaves at **Clarendon Street** in **Preston.** Built of honey-coloured concrete blocks, with panels of a ribbed texture set back behind plain pilasters which support a projecting and battlemented parapet, and with the 'mihrab' (the niche which indicates to the congregation the direction of Mecca) projecting from the back wall, it reflects in its form the Arabic origins of Islam and makes a notable, and welcome, contribution to the cultural and architectural richness of Lancashire's heritage.

There was a time, not very long ago, when even to listen to another person's view of religion, without seeking to persuade him of the rightness of one's own perceptions, was regarded as a form of culpable weakness, if not of back-sliding in the faith of one's fathers. Since the War we have had to come to terms with the fact that we live in a multi-racial world and that our country is now multi-cultural; most of us now accept that (as the Quakers say) there is 'that of God in every man' and that variety and diversity lead to an enrichment of human experience. **Lancaster University** is a multi-national community – a world in miniature – and this is the message

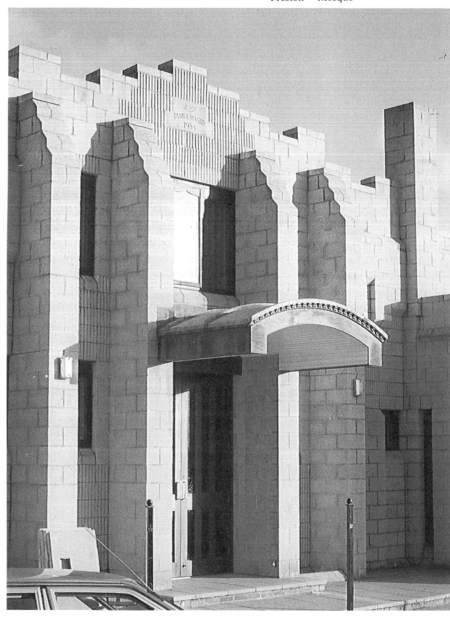

Lancaster University
– Chaplaincy Centre

of the **Chaplaincy Centre** there, which was designed by two Roman Catholic architects, Gerald Cassidy and Bernard Ashton, and opened in 1969. In its plan it has the form of a clover leaf, a much-used symbol of the Christian perception of God as three persons in one; but while two of the circular rooms are dedicated to a Roman Catholic chapel and an Anglican and Free Church chapel respectively, the largest provides spaces for Muslims and Jews to worship in, and for other people of other faiths, or none, to meet, to discuss, to sit in quietness. This more open-minded approach to one's neighbour and his God is reflected in the internal plan of the building, which allows the main chapels to be opened up to a central concourse for ecumenical acts of worship, and also in the fact that the tallest of the Centre's three spires does not carry a cross, but merely points upwards – to symbolise, perhaps, the importance of searching rather than certainty, of love of one's neighbour as much as love of God.

I have sought to bring my anthology up to date because, as a Conservation Officer, I am as much concerned about the quality of new developments as about the protection of fine old buildings. Conservation work – as I

understand it and try to practise it – is not a nostalgic, but a forward-looking activity; it is concerned with architectural quality rather than antiquarianism, with historic buildings and not merely old ones. Every generation of Lancastrians for the past eight hundred years has left an interesting and often moving memorial of its qualities in the buildings of its day which have survived to form our architectural heritage – even though these buildings were, in terms of their quality, the exceptions rather than the rule at the time when they were built. There is no prior reason why our generation should not also make a fine and interesting contribution for the people of the future, but this will not happen automatically.

It has never been easy to create a good building, one which meets the traditional three-fold criteria: convenience of plan, structural solidity, and attractive and appropriate appearance; it is even more difficult now in the North of England, where there is an understandably strong temptation to welcome any development which creates work as a good development, regardless of other considerations. One needs a developer who is prepared to strike a socially responsible balance between his wholly

165

legitimate private wish to make a commercially viable investment and the equally valid community requirement that he should not do so at the expense of public amenity. One needs a designer of more than average competence to produce a convenient plan, appropriate façade and well-designed details; then one needs good-quality materials and skilled craftsmen to assemble them. Only when all these ingredients are in the mix does one have a chance of seeing a fine building emerge from the scaffolding.

These conditions have, however, been fulfilled often enough since the War for me to be able to claim with confidence that the Art of Architecture is not dead in the late twentieth century, and that our age too is making its contribution to our children's architectural heritage.

INDEX OF PLACES AND BUILDINGS